VGM Opportunities Series

OPPORTUNITIES IN
EDUCATION
CAREERS

**Mary McGowan
Marjorie Eberts
Margaret Gisler**

VGM Career Horizons
NTC/Contemporary Publishing Group

Library of Congress Cataloging-in-Publication Data

Eberts, Marjorie.
    Opportunities in education careers / Marjorie Eberts and Mary McGowan.
        p.   cm. — (VGM opportunities series)
    ISBN 0-658-00618-5 (c) — ISBN 0-658-00619-3 (p)
        1. Education—Vocational guidance—United States.   I. McGowan, Mary.
II. Title.   III. Series.
LB1775.2 .E22   2000
371.1'0023—dc21   99-53680
                                                                                CIP

Cover photograph: © PhotoDisc, Inc.

Published by VGM Career Horizons
A division of NTC/Contemporary Publishing Group, Inc.
4255 West Touhy Avenue, Lincolnwood (Chicago), Illinois 60712-1975 U.S.A.
Copyright © 2000 by NTC/Contemporary Publishing Group, Inc.
Printed in the United States of America
International Standard Book Number: 0-658-00618-5 (cloth)
                                                            0-658-00619-3 (paper)

(01 02 03 04 05 LB 15 14 13 12 11 10 9   8   7   6   5   4   3   2

DEDICATION

To all the educators who have guided this generation of children through school and especially to Nancylee Buckley, Fred Chandler, and Pennie Needham, who have been outstanding teachers, counselors, and administrators.

CONTENTS

ABOUT THE AUTHORS

The three authors have collectively written twenty-six career books. They are also experienced educators with many years of teaching experience in schools from kindergarten through college. Margaret Gisler, who has taught in kindergarten, elementary school, and college, is currently working in special education. Marjorie Eberts has taught in high school and college, and Mary McGowan has taught in middle school. Marjorie Eberts and Margaret Gisler also write a syndicated education column, "Dear Teacher," which appears in newspapers across the country. Recently, they have become the education experts on the Family Education web site.

Mary McGowan and Marjorie Eberts hold bachelor's and master's degrees from Stanford University. Margaret Gisler received her bachelor's degree at Ball State University. Both Marjorie Eberts and Margaret Gisler have master's and education specialists degrees in education.

FOREWORD

Education is arguably one of the most important and rewarding careers one can pursue in life. No one can survive in today's world without an education. With an education, people will flourish. In fact, one can say that the more education a person receives, the better he or she will succeed in a given profession or pursuit.

Education provides not only the basic skills needed for everyday activities, it also provides the highly specialized training needed in order to prepare for the complex and technical jobs and careers that sometimes seem to spring up overnight.

But apart from preparation for jobs and careers, an education offers something even more important; it helps people get more out of their lives. Teachers and others working in education-related areas are there because they understand this. They, themselves, have experienced what a good education can do for a person, and they are caring and intelligent enough to want to provide the same for others.

Are you one of these people? Do you have the desire to help people grow intellectually and make something of their lives? Do you want people to get the most enjoyment out of their lives? If so, this book is for you. We hope the information you find here starts you on a journey toward a career in education.

The Editors
VGM Career Books

CHAPTER 1

EXPLORING THE OPPORTUNITIES IN EDUCATION

Education is not the filling of a pail, but the lighting of a fire.

William Butler Yeats

A modern society cannot exist without education. Education helps us acquire the skills needed in everyday life from reading the newspaper to handling money. It provides us with the special training required for so many careers. And it makes our lives richer as it expands our knowledge and understanding of the world around us. While much education takes place outside of schools, teachers and schools have the major responsibility of educating people in this country, whether they are young children in preschool, college students studying for bachelor's degrees, or workers upgrading their professional skills.

THE HISTORY OF EDUCATION

In prehistoric societies, young boys and girls got their practical education in the ways to hunt, gather food, and construct shelters by working closely with those who possessed these essential skills. Formal education didn't really begin until 5,000 years ago, when a system of writing both words and numbers was invented.

1

Of course, education then was nothing like it is today. For one thing, it was only for boys, and it consisted largely of copying literary selections and business accounts. The first giant step forward in education occurred in ancient Greece. Boys began to study reading, writing, arithmetic, music, and dancing; however, instead of going to a school, they would go to different teachers for each subject. It was during this time that Aristotle, Plato, and Socrates emerged as great teachers and philosophers.

The first large-scale education system evolved in the ancient Roman Empire around 100 B.C. Although the system was modeled on Greek education, schooling also was provided for girls, and students learned to read and write both Latin and Greek. There was even a secondary system of schools that let boys between the ages of ten and fifteen continue their education. During the Middle Ages, the Christian church controlled most formal education. At first it was for boys intending to enter religious life, but later on schools for boys of wealthy and noble families were established at churches and monasteries.

During the 1100s, universities first emerged. In Northern Europe they were really corporations of scholars who charged a fee to educate students. In Southern Europe, the universities were guilds of students who hired the teachers. By 1500, today's great universities of Cambridge, Oxford, Paris, and Salamanca had been founded, as well as primary schools for children of the lower classes. About 1440, education was suddenly revolutionized by the invention of the printing press, which let more and more students have low-cost books.

American Education

When the colonists came to America, they set up schools like they had known in Europe. Most children, however, did not attend school but served apprenticeships to learn a trade. The first public schools in America were established by law in Massachusetts in 1647. Both boys and girls could attend these schools. In the 1700s, secondary schools, called academies, began to appear and offer practical courses. Compulsory education was required in a few states by the late 1800s; however, it was not required in all the states until 1918. The curriculum in schools broadened in the 1900s from the 3R's to include such subjects as history, geography, and science. Today, the American education system has expanded to include preschools and kindergartens; elementary, middle, and secondary schools; community colleges, colleges, and universities; trade schools; adult education programs; and specialty schools instructing people of all ages in a variety of skills from mathematics to karate.

AN AMAZING VARIETY OF JOBS

As new inventions and technology are rapidly changing today's world, being educated is more important than ever before. Education is a career field in which individuals can make an important contribution to people of all ages. You do not have to be a teacher to work in the world of education. There are many other careers that will let you support education. Here is a quick look at the careers that will be described in this book.

Teaching Preschool to High School

Classroom teachers are the individuals who play the greatest role in passing the culture to the next generation. They introduce children in elementary school to reading, numbers, language, science, social studies, and the arts and help students in secondary school delve more deeply into these subjects. This is an enormous profession totaling close to five million people. Not only does teaching require an ability to work with young people, it is essential for teachers who work in public schools to be licensed. You may wish to consider teaching as a career choice because it is a rewarding profession that would let you see students develop new skills and gain an appreciation of knowledge.

Teaching in Special Areas

Some children simply cannot handle school because of significant physical and/or mental disabilities. Special education teachers have the challenge of helping these students. This is a fairly new profession of approximately five hundred thousand teachers, and it is growing rapidly. There are even shortages of special education teachers in many school districts. If you decide to become a special education teacher, you will need to hold a teaching license as well as special licensure in this field.

Jobs in Advising and Counseling Students

It is important for students to get the best possible education. However, personal problems sometimes interfere. At other times, students need special information about what classes to take, what career opportunities are right for them, and what colleges are good choices for them. There are also times when students have problems with teachers, their schoolwork, or classmates. When students need advice or counseling, the individuals who help them are the school counselors, deans, psychologists, and nurses. Here is a way that you can be involved in students' education without being a teacher.

Opportunities in School Administration

Schools don't just run themselves. They need administrators to handle their day-to-day operation as well as to manage each school district. Those who work in elementary and secondary schools have a very hands-on role in the education of children and work closely with their teachers and parents. Administrators at the district level are concerned with budgets, hiring personnel, directing subject area programs, overseeing transportation, and setting the overall standards and policies of the schools under their jurisdiction. Most administrators begin their careers as teachers, although it is not essential for a great number of positions.

Jobs at Colleges and Universities

Teaching is the number-one job at all colleges and universities. Beyond choosing to teach at this level, there are opportunities for jobs as administrators and support personnel in many areas. You might want to work in the admissions office, athletic department, financial aid office, or in the public relations, budget, development, security, and buildings or grounds departments. While positions such as college or university president, dean, and department head require experience in the education arena, other jobs do not. Most individuals who work at a school, however, will have an intense interest in promoting its success.

Jobs at Trade Schools and Community Colleges

An amazing number of students now are preparing themselves for careers as unusual as acupuncturist and deep-sea diver or as common as plumber and welder at trade schools and community colleges. Here is an opportunity to be involved in teaching a subject in which you are an expert without having to hold educational degrees or licenses. There are also jobs in the administration and operation of these schools.

Trade schools usually concentrate on teaching a particular job skill such as court reporting, hairstyling, or truck driving. On the other hand, community colleges are more like colleges and universities in that their focus is typically on offering academic courses, but they also have many programs leading to licensing or certification in a great number of careers.

Jobs with Departments of Education at Federal, State, and County Levels

Students are entitled to a free and appropriate public school education in elementary and secondary schools. While local communities exercise considerable control over their schools, county, state, and federal departments of education also play an important role. County departments of education largely provide services and information to school districts. State departments of education set broad outlines of what will be taught in the state and provide financing and services to school districts. The federal department of education distributes grant money to individuals, schools, and states; collects statistics; provides information; and makes sure that all students have an equal educational opportunity. Within all these departments of education, there are jobs for both educators and support staff.

Education Researchers and Consultants

School districts have questions: Is our new reading program effective? Has the high school block schedule plan improved students' grades. States want to know if reducing class size in the primary grades has lowered the retention rate. The federal government is eager to know if a program to serve breakfast in elementary schools has improved attendance. The answers to all of these questions about what works in education are sought by educational researchers, who are typically affiliated with universities.

When school districts, departments of education, and even parents are not sure about what to do in a given situation, they often hire educational consultants to advise them. Educational consultants perform such tasks as helping school districts select the best design for a new school, finding suitable candidates for administrative positions, and helping high school students choose an appropriate college. While being a researcher or consultant requires knowledge of the educational system, each job also requires special research and investigative skills.

Learning and Test Preparation Centers and Tutoring

Approximately 40 percent of all parents believe that their children need outside help in order to succeed in today's schools. This belief sends tens of thousands of students after school each day to learning and test preparation centers and tutors. Many learning centers are part of large national chains with positions for administrators and part-time teachers. Tutors are usually self-employed. They either have students come to their homes, or they go to the homes of their clients. Test preparation centers may be part of national chains or independent centers. They employ administrative staff as well as experts at taking college admissions tests (SAT and ACT) and various examinations to enter graduate school and certain professions.

MORE GREAT JOBS IN EDUCATION

Admittedly, being a teacher is the most popular job in education. At the same time, there are many other job options for those who wish to have a career in education. Individuals are needed to create tests and administer testing programs. As technology comes to schools, computer experts are required to set up and run computer networks. All of the textbooks used in schools are written by authors and sold to schools by salespeople who work for large and small publishing firms. There are web companies on the Internet that provide advice to parents, students, and teachers. Librarians run school libraries. Secretaries are the heart of many schools. Plus, professional organizations and unions have large staffs serving the interests of their members. Talk to educators, and you will find even more jobs than are described in this book.

FOR MORE INFORMATION

The more you know about education, the more likely you will find the appropriate niche in this very large career field. Working as a volunteer at a school or as a teacher's aide will allow you to observe many careers in education. Also, you will find the following career books helpful in your search for a job in education:

Careers in Education (VGM Career Horizons) lists dozens of jobs in the educational field, along with the education and training required for these jobs.

Real People Working in Education (VGM Career Horizons) will help you discover what it's like to work in education by reading directly about practicing professionals. It will reveal how they got started, spend their days, and feel about their work.

Resumes for Education Careers (VGM Career Horizons) will help you learn how to write a strong resume as well as see the backgrounds people are bringing to this field.

CHAPTER 2

TEACHING PRESCHOOL TO HIGH SCHOOL

Children enter preschool not knowing how to read, write, or do arithmetic and then graduate from high school many years later with a solid core of knowledge that will let them lead useful and rewarding lives. The growth of their intellectual powers has been fostered by working with teachers. The preschool teacher begins the process by teaching children to rhyme words and count; then the kindergarten teacher introduces them to letters and numbers, so they will be ready to handle first grade. With each passing year, children acquire a broader and deeper base of knowledge because teachers help them learn.

More people belong to the teaching profession than any other profession in the world. Included in this group are many well-known people. Did you realize that Bill Cosby, the television star of several shows, has a doctorate in education? While Bill was working on his doctorate, he studied the uses and effects of electronic devices, including television, on children's education. Bill is still involved in education as he uses his acting skills on television to teach young children. You may have seen him on *The Electric Company* teaching young children to read, or on *Sesame Street* teaching children to say their letters and numbers. Even his cartoons "Fat Albert" and the "Cosby Kids" have an educational message. Look at the following list of other well-known people who have spent all or part of their lives teaching.

Sir Isaac Newton (English mathematician and physicist)
Mary McLeod Bethune (American educator)
Maria Montessori (Italian physician and educator)
John Dewey (American philosopher and educator)
Christa McAuliffe (American educator who died in the *Challanger* explosion in 1989)
Lyndon Baines Johnson (36th President of the United States)
Barbara Jordan (first black woman from a Southern state to serve in the U.S. Congress)
Theodore Hesburgh (president of Notre Dame University from 1952–1987)
Alexander Melville Bell (father of Alexander Graham Bell)
Annie Sullivan (Helen Keller's teacher)

PRESCHOOL TEACHERS

Just imagine being a child's first teacher! When children enter preschool, they are only three or four years old and have no idea of what school is like, except possibly from playing school with older brothers and sisters or neighborhood children. Preschool teachers have the task of introducing young children to school and preparing them for kindergarten. This doesn't mean teaching them to read or write or do workbook activities. Instead, it means helping children learn to function in the classroom setting. They must be taught to listen attentively, to solve problems, to manipulate their hands effectively, to socialize with their classmates, to express themselves clearly, and to take care of their basic needs. Simultaneously, the preschool teacher must fan their desire to learn through interesting activities for groups and individuals. Good preschool teachers give young children a big boost up the school ladder of success. It is an excellent career consideration for pro-spective teachers who especially like young children.

Education and Training Requirements

Where preschool teachers work largely determines the educa-tion background they will need. Most states require teachers to have a certificate to teach in a public preschool. These teachers usually have a four-year college degree in child development or early childhood education plus the necessary licenses. Preschool teachers at private schools usually face less stringent require-ments. They may hold an associate's degree in early childhood education. Some enter the field through the Child Development Associate (CDA) program offered by the Council for Early Child-hood Professional Recognition. In addition, preschool teachers can get training through the American Montessori Society, which offers many different programs.

Attributes

Preschool teachers need to have an excellent understanding of children, how they develop and what their abilities are at each age level. They have to have this knowledge to create age-appropriate activities. They also must be willing to act not only as a teacher but also as nurse, referee for fights, a playground director, a parent, and a friend. Successful preschool teachers have a high energy level, a pleasant-sounding voice, creativity, patience, and the abil-ity to keep cool when things go wrong.

Salaries and Fringe Benefits

Preschool teachers' salaries are typically based on their educa-tion level and the number of years of teaching experience they have. The rate of pay is often only an hourly wage. In general, the pay for preschool teachers is fairly low. However, those working in public schools will typically earn slightly higher wages.

Benefits for preschool teachers, such as health insurance and paid vacations, vary widely, with some schools providing good benefits and others offering no benefits. Teachers at this level, however, work relatively short hours. There is also the added bonus of having time-off for all major holidays plus a long summer vacation.

Working as a Preschool Teacher

Cathy Johnson is a lead teacher in a preschool where she has the responsibility of selecting what will be taught in the classroom, planning how it will be taught, and teaching the lesson. She doesn't work alone but has two aides who provide her with support in the classroom. Besides teaching, Cathy regularly holds conferences with parents and writes notes every day letting them know how their children are doing. Lead teachers also must handle the paperwork involved in running a class.

No two days are alike for Cathy. Three days a week, she teaches a class of four-year-olds. On two of those days, the children attend school from 9:00 to 11:30 A.M., while the third day is extended until 2:00 P.M. and the children bring their lunches to school. One day a week, she teaches a morning class of two-year-olds from 9:30 to 11:30 and a kindergarten enrichment program from 12:15 to 2:30. Cathy has one day off a week, in addition to weekends.

The preschool where Cathy teaches is a private school. It does not require its teachers to have a degree in early childhood education, but they must have a teaching degree, and one in elementary education is preferred. Cathy has a master's degree in early childhood education and a kindergarten endorsement.

Job Opportunities

One of the fastest growing segments of employment in education is preschool teaching. More and more young children are now attending school earlier and earlier because both parents are working. In addition, the attention being focused on the problem of poor compensation for teachers is resulting in slightly higher wages and improved benefits.

KINDERGARTEN TEACHERS

It has been said that all the important things people need to know in life are learned in kindergarten. This is where they learn how to share, respect others, tell the truth, and do their best at all times. What is learned and experienced during the early years can definitely shape children's views of themselves and the world and affect their success or failure in school, work, and life. Unquestionably, kindergarten teachers play a vital role in the lives of their students. It is challenging for them to provide interesting, exciting, and motivating ideas that will inspire their students to learn and keep on learning each day.

More and more kindergarten teachers are working in full-day programs. In half-day programs, they will usually teach both a morning and an afternoon session. In some school districts, kindergarten teachers will teach one group of students all day on Monday and Wednesday and half day on Friday, and another group on Tuesday and Thursday and the other half of the day on Friday. In the first semester, kindergarten programs are more like those in preschool; however, in the second semester, attention is focused on preparing the children for first grade.

Education Requirements

Kindergarten teachers are considered elementary school teachers and will need to meet the same general requirements. Although the requirements for teaching in elementary school will vary from state to state, all teachers in public schools need to be licensed. To be licensed, they will need to earn a bachelor's degree and complete an approved teacher training program with a prescribed number of subject and education credits and supervised teaching. Licensing requirements are becoming stiffer. Some states even require a minimum grade point average, while almost all states now are requiring applicants for teacher licenses to be tested for competency in basic skills such as reading and writing, teaching skills, or subject matter proficiency. Plus, many states are starting to require teachers to demonstrate satisfactory teaching performance over an extended period of time to obtain full licensure. Teachers may be licensed to teach the early childhood grades, usually preschool through grade three; the elementary grades, which are grades one through six or eight; or the middle grades of five through eight. Because most school districts have continuing education requirements, teachers usually work toward master's degrees.

Many states have reciprocity agreements that make it easier for teachers who are licensed in one state to become licensed in another. In addition there are emergency licenses for individuals with bachelor's degrees who do not meet all requirements for a license when school districts cannot find enough licensed personnel to employ. In some of these programs, teachers begin working quickly under provisional licensing; they receive regular licenses after working one or two years under the close supervision of experienced educators and taking education courses outside of school hours.

In the last few years, the National Board for Professional Teaching Standards has begun to offer voluntary national certification to teachers who have proved their aptitude by compiling a portfolio of their classroom work and by passing a test of their teaching knowledge. Being nationally certified can make it easier to obtain employment in another state and also may lead to higher salaries as well as more bonuses.

Salaries and Fringe Benefits

How much money elementary school teachers make depends largely on where they work, the degrees they hold, and the number of years they have taught. While the average salary for teachers at this level is currently slightly more than $37,000 a year, it is important to remember that beginning teachers often have salaries in the low- to mid-$20,000 range. Then with each year of experience, their salaries climb according to the salary scale of the school district. Private school teachers generally earn less than public school teachers.

More than half of all public school teachers belong to unions— mainly the American Federation of Teachers and the National Education Association. The unions bargain with school systems over wages, hours, and the terms and conditions of employment. In many schools, teachers receive extra pay for coaching sports and working with students in extracurricular activities. Some teachers earn extra income during the summer working in the school system or in other jobs.

Public school teachers have benefits packages that typically include health and life insurance. Furthermore, they have paid sick leave, and most school districts also allow leave days for conducting personal business, handling family emergencies, and serving as jurors. Most public school teachers are obliged to participate in a retirement program under either a state teachers' retirement system or a state public employees' retirement system. Both teacher and school district contribute to retirement programs. Some of these programs offer good retirement benefits. Unfortunately, these benefits cannot be transferred from state to state.

Unique Benefits

There are certain benefits that are unique to the teaching profession. Their work year is much shorter than any other profession, averaging only 180 days or approximately 36 weeks. While this traditionally included a long summer break, the advent of the year-round school in many districts has resulted in more frequent breaks during the school year. Many teachers now work for forty-five days (nine weeks) and then have fifteen days (three weeks) off.

Teachers also enjoy a certain amount of job security because of tenure laws. These laws prevent teachers from being fired without just cause and due process. Teachers may obtain tenure after a probationary period, typically three years. During that time, administrators frequently visit their classrooms to evaluate whether the teachers are doing a satisfactory job.

Working as a Kindergarten Teacher

Annette Saint Clair was well-prepared when she began her teaching career as a kindergarten teacher. She had just graduated from college and had a bachelor' degree in elementary education as well as a master's degree, and held a K–12 teaching license. It was an extremely challenging position as the brand-new school where she was to teach would not open until almost the end of the year. Her classroom for thirty-six children was an eleven-foot-by-twenty-foot room with adult-sized furnishings in a church. Painting activities were done in the hallway, and the children laid down on pews for their rest period. The principal was not an on-site administrator because the school's classrooms were scattered throughout the community, so Annette had no immediate supervisor to rely on for help on a day-to-day basis. It was at this job, however, that Annette had her first look at the administrative side of education when she served as a mentor to an inexperienced teacher during the second semester. In Chapter 5, you will discover how Annette climbed the education ladder to an administrative position.

Job Opportunities

The employment of kindergarten and elementary school teachers is expected to grow about as fast as the average for all occupations through the year 2005. The number of elementary school job openings will increase substantially from the mid-1990s to 2005 as a large number of teachers retire. How many teachers will actually be employed depends on state and local expenditures for education. Pressure from taxpayers to reduce expenditures could result in fewer teachers being hired; conversely pressure to improve the quality of education, such as reducing class size, could result in more job openings.

ELEMENTARY SCHOOL TEACHERS

Elementary school teachers have the task of introducing children to academics as well as to guiding their emotional, social, physical, and mental development. In the primary grades, one through three, emphasis is on the traditional 3R's. As the children proceed through elementary school, they also are taught in the content areas of history, science, health, and English.

Elementary school teachers spend most of their time in a classroom with a class ranging in size from fifteen to thirty children. The school may have special teachers who will take their students for music, art, physical education, and library. Classroom teachers can use this time for preparing lessons or grading papers. Although most elementary school teachers instruct one class of children in several subjects, in some schools two or more teachers teach as a team and are jointly responsible for a group of students in at least one subject. A small but growing number of teachers instruct multilevel classrooms, that is, students at several different learning levels together in one classroom. Elementary school teachers also are expected to supervise their classes on the playground and may have additional duties supervising lunchrooms, halls, and bus loading and unloading. Including activities outside of the classroom, many teachers work more than forty hours per week.

Elementary school teachers plan lessons, prepare tests, grade papers, make out report cards, meet with parents, and attend faculty meetings and conferences. In addition, they assign lessons, give tests, hear oral presentations, and oversee special projects. Teachers also have the job of keeping order in their classrooms and diagnosing and correcting learning problems.

Children don't just learn from books. Teachers must know how to use films, slides, overhead projectors, and the latest technology in their teaching. The new classroom tool is the computer. Teachers are having their students use the Internet for individual research projects, information gathering, and interactive learning experiences. When the astronauts go into space or a biologist visits the Amazon, classes can go on-line not only to see what these professionals are doing but ask them questions. Many teachers also have helped their classes build web pages to describe classroom activities. Besides using the computer with their students, teachers now are using computers to record grades and for other administrative and clerical functions.

Being an elementary school teacher isn't an easy job. Teachers are on their feet for many hours each day. They do not have much contact with adults during working hours. And on a bad day, teaching can drain their energy and challenge them to stay even-tempered.

(For educational requirements and salary information, as well as other unique benefits, for elementary school teachers, see discussion of kindergarten teachers above.)

Working as an Elementary School Teacher

Karl Knerr is a fifth-grade teacher who likes his job because it has so much variety. Besides being a teacher, he also is a communicator, a planner, and a problem solver. Karl especially appreciates the training he gained from both his undergraduate and graduate classes in education, as he uses those skills on the job every day. He begins his day at school by greeting and visiting with the students as they enter the classroom. Then the students get organized for the day and listen to the morning announcements. The class works on math and language arts before lunch, and science, health, and social studies after lunch. And sometime during the day, Karl always reads to them. When his students leave the classroom for a special class such as art, music, or physical education, Karl prepares lessons and activities, grades papers, communicates with parents, and meets with other professionals and the principal. At the end of the day, Karl stays on to prepare for the next day and to grade papers. Then he travels to the high school to coach track.

Working as a Music Teacher

Some teachers concentrate on teaching children a specific subject in elementary school. For example, many elementary schools have reading, music, art, and physical education teachers on their teaching staffs. These teachers generally are required to have bachelor's degrees in education with special training in their subject area. They will typically hold elementary school credentials with an endorsement in their special area.

Julia Scherer is a music teacher at a K–5 elementary school. She graduated from college with a bachelor's degree in music education and has earned a master's degree in music and taken additional courses. As an elementary music specialist, Julia teaches general music classes that feature instruction in vocal music, composers, music reading, instruments of the orchestra, music appreciation, and playing the recorder.

Julia has to make lesson plans, take attendance, and give grades, just like other elementary schoolteachers. Plus, in the course of a week, she will see every student in the school, which means getting to know hundreds of students. Besides her normal teaching duties, Julia directs the students in one or more musical programs each year, which are presented in the evening to parents.

MIDDLE SCHOOL AND JUNIOR HIGH SCHOOL TEACHERS

Middle school and junior high school teachers work with children as they are starting to cross the bridge from childhood to adolescence. Rather than teach a wide variety of subjects, these teachers usually concentrate on teaching within a single subject area such as mathematics, English, science, social studies, reading, art, music, and physical education. Teachers at this level will teach five or more classes in their subject area and have a free period during the day to devote to preparation. For each class, they will write lesson plans, make and correct tests, collect homework, and contact parents when it is necessary. They will be required to perform routine bookkeeping tasks like taking attendance for every class and keeping track of issued textbooks. Beside classroom-oriented work, many middle and junior high school teachers are involved in supervising extracurricular activities.

Middle school and junior high school teachers may hold either general elementary or secondary credentials. Preparation for teaching at this level will vary. In general, course work will include education courses dealing with psychology, tests and measurements, methods of teaching in the special subject area, and student teaching in that area. In addition, college courses in the subject area will give prospective teachers a solid knowledge of the subject they teach.

Teachers at this grade level can climb the career ladder to become department heads. In this position they are responsible for all the teachers teaching the same general subject, such as English, mathematics, or science. They teach some classes and help the other teachers in the department decide what is to be taught in each class, as well as help them with any problems. At many schools they also are involved in rating teachers' performance.

Being a junior high or middle school teacher is like being both an elementary school and a senior high school teacher. The children receive more guidance than high school students, but at the same time they have separate teachers for each subject.

Working as a Middle School Teacher

Titus Exum teaches eighth grade American history. He has a bachelor's degree in elementary education and a master's in school administration and supervision. He holds elementary credentials in Missouri and Alaska. To obtain his present job, Titus had to take the National Teacher Examinations.

Titus works as a part of a five-person teaching team. Each teacher teaches only one subject; however, they work together to plan assemblies, select guest speakers, arrange field trips, organize field days, and handle other situations involving all of the eighth graders. Titus finds that the hardest part of his job is motivating those students who are not interested in learning history. He believes that he has had a successful day when the students in all his classes actively participate in a class or group project, a class discussion, or a multilevel assignment. Then he feels that he can actually see the students learning in his classes.

Working as a Junior High School Teacher

Jane Jones is an English teacher with bachelor's and master's degrees in English literature. She even spent almost a year studying at Oxford University. While Jane's knowledge of English is outstanding, she never has had an education course and is teaching on a two-year temporary license. She was given the license with the condition that she take at least one class toward obtaining a license in the next two years.

Jane's first assignment was to teach five regular classes and one honors English class. This was not an easy job for someone who was an inexperienced teacher. Furthermore, the school did not have a mentor program, so there was really no one directly responsible for helping her. Fortunately, she was part of a team composed of a math, a biology, and a history teacher who met each day for forty-five minutes of planning to formulate shared assignments. For example, in a unit on Gregor Johann Mendel, the biology teacher would stress genetics, the math teacher would introduce probability, the history teacher would examine the time period, and Jane would assign reading on biographical information.

The team not only assisted Jane in planning classroom assignments, they also gave her valuable help on effective disciplinary techniques to use in the classroom. And when parents asked for a parent/teacher conference, all the team members would attend.

Jane soon learned to organize her classes in a very structured way so the students would know what to expect each day. Every session began with a short five- to ten-minute silent writing time to hone the students' skills in this area. The remainder of the class time was devoted to concentrating on literature or grammar. By the end of the year, Jane felt at home in the classroom and was eager to begin work on obtaining a teacher's license.

HIGH SCHOOL TEACHERS

High school teachers help students delve more deeply into subjects. Most specialize in a specific subject, such as English, French, mathematics, or biology. They do not usually teach just one subject but will teach a variety of related courses. For example, a teacher in a history department might teach one or more classes in American history, a class in American social problems, and two classes in world geography. In the same way, a science teacher might teach both chemistry and physics, and an art teacher might have both drawing and craft classes.

High school teachers usually stay in the same classroom throughout the day and teach four or five classes lasting from forty to fifty-five minutes each. Some schools, however, are switching to block schedule plans, in which teachers have fewer classes lasting from eighty to one hundred minutes and see the same students every other day instead of on a daily basis. With either scheduling plan, most teachers have a free period that can be used to prepare for their classes. Besides duties related directly to teaching, high school teachers may find themselves supervising a homeroom, study hall, or a lunchroom. And they will need to spend considerable time conferring with students and parents, participating on various committees, attending meetings, chaperoning and supervising school functions, and directing extracurricular activities. For example, teachers may teach English all day, and then work for weeks after school helping the drama club produce a play, or they may find themselves teaching five classes of chemistry and then coaching the girls' soccer team.

Because high school teachers are subject specialists, they have the opportunity to share their personal interests with their students. Also, many enjoy working with students who are generally more independent, sophisticated, and self-reliant than younger students. Furthermore, most high school students understand the importance of doing well in school.

Salaries

The average salaries of public school secondary teachers are slightly higher than those for elementary schoolteachers with their salaries averaging close to $39,000 a year. Their benefits, however, are comparable.

Working as a Music Teacher

Thomas Dick, an accomplished musician, made the decision in college to become a teacher and help young people appreciate music rather than be a performer. Since completing his bachelor's degree in music education, Thomas has taught at three high schools, obtaining his master's degree in music education along the way. In his present job, he is the director of the orchestra at a large suburban high school where he teaches four periods of strings and one period of wind and percussion each day. During a typical strings class, he will begin by having the students play scales for intonation, quality of sound, and technique. Most of the period then will be spent working on problems with current pieces, with some time devoted to sight reading and the teaching of musical terms, abbreviations, and signs.

The day is long for a high school music teacher. Four days a week Thomas supervises rehearsals of different sections of the orchestra after school, then every Tuesday evening he holds a three-hour rehearsal of performance and possible contest pieces to discover problems that the students can work on at home and in their sections. Thomas receives a stipend for the work he does with students beyond the regular school day, as most high school music teachers do. During the school year, he will be the guest conductor for junior and senior high school orchestras and act as a judge at several music contests. He also finds time to serve on the board of the state school music association. In the summer, Thomas will often act as the orchestra director of a summer music camp.

Working as an English Teacher

Giving students objectives before each reading assignment is Felice Knarr's way of developing critical readers in her twelfth-grade English literature classes at a private school. In August, before school starts, Felice charts out her course of study for the entire school year. She reads every book that the students will be reading so that she knows how long each reading assignment should take. This is not the only time Felice reads the material that will be assigned to her students. Before each reading assignment is made, she rereads the material to develop the objectives for her lesson plans. Beyond all the reading that Felice does in her preparation, she also spends six to eight hours a week grading the essays and compositions of her one hundred students. This does not include the additional time spent in grading vocabulary, spelling, and short writing assignments and on reading professional journals.

Job Opportunities

The job market for secondary school teachers varies widely by geographic area and by subject specialty. Many inner cities with their high crime rates, high poverty rates, and overcrowded conditions as well as rural areas in remote locations paying relatively low salaries have difficulty attracting enough teachers. Job prospects should continue to be better in these areas than in suburban districts. Currently, many school districts have difficulty hiring qualified teachers in some subjects: mathematics, science (especially chemistry and physics), bilingual education, and computer science. At the same time, there is an abundance of qualified teachers in English, art, physical education, and social studies. Teachers who are geographically mobile and who obtain licensure in more than one subject should have a distinct advantage in finding a job on the secondary level.

FOR MORE INFORMATION

One of the best ways to actually learn what being a teacher is like is by working as a teacher's assistant or tutor. Such experiences should help you decide if this is a profession that would be right for you.

A list of institutions with accredited teacher education programs can be obtained from: National Council for Accreditation of Teacher Education, 2010 Massachusetts Avenue NW, Suite 500, Washington, DC 20036.

For information on voluntary national teacher certification requirements, contact: National Board for Professional Teaching Standards, 26555 Evergreen Road, Suite 400, Southfield, MI 48076.

For information about eligibility requirements and a description of the Child Development Associate (CDA) credential, write: Early Childhood Profession Recognition, 1718 Connecticut Avenue NW, Suite 500, Washington, DC 20013.

CHAPTER 3

TEACHING IN SPECIAL AREAS

Fifty years ago, when people talked about being a teacher, most thought only of working in a traditional classroom. Some other teaching opportunities existed in state schools for the blind and deaf and programs for those who had significant physical and mental disabilities. In recent years, legislation and public interest has focused on helping students who were having difficulty keeping up with their peers in mainstream classrooms. Teachers are now working in special areas to help students overcome learning disabilities and learn English as a second language. At the same time, teaching jobs have emerged to help gifted and talented students who are not being challenged in the regular classroom setting. Most of these special areas are growing rapidly, and many school districts report shortages of qualified teachers.

SPECIAL EDUCATION TEACHERS

Special education teachers work with students who have problems learning in the regular classroom from preschool through high school. These students may have learning disabilities; serious emotional disturbances; mental retardation; visual, hearing, speech, or orthopedic impairments; autism; traumatic brain injuries; or multiple disabilities. By law, schools are required to develop an Individualized Education Program (IEP) for each special education student. These programs set personalized goals for students and are tailored to their individual learning styles and abilities. Special education teachers are involved in the creation, implementation, and annual review of these programs.

Special education teachers work in a variety of settings. Some work in their own classrooms and teach classes composed entirely of special education students; others work as special education resource teachers and offer individualized help to students in general education classrooms; and others teach alongside general education teachers in classrooms composed of both general and special education students.

Job Requirements

You will need to have a bachelor's degree and a teacher's license in order to become a special education teacher. In addition, most states will require you to have a special education license. Some even require you to have a master's degree in special education. Currently, national certification standards for special education teachers are being developed by the National Board for Professional Teaching Standards.

Special education teachers need to be "people" persons as so much of their job involves interacting with others (teachers, parents, psychologists, students). They also need to be patient, able to motivate students, understand students' special needs, and accept differences in others. At the same time, they must be creative in developing programs to reach students with very diverse needs.

Salaries

Salaries of special education teachers follow the same scale as those for general education teachers. See Chapter 2 for average salaries.

Working as a Resource Specialist

Sandi Harris is a resource specialist who has her own classroom in a large high school where she works with students who have learning disabilities. When students enter her classroom, several introductory assignments for them to do are already on the board. Typically, they will have to correct a sentence, do a geography related assignment, and complete an analogy. All of the students then participate in a structured spelling, reading, and writing program that Sandi teaches to improve these skills. For the rest of her time with a class, Sandi works with individual students helping them improve academic and study skills and handle assignments from their regular classrooms.

Much of the remaining two hours of Sandi's workday is devoted to handling IEP's. After a student has been evaluated and found to have a learning disability, she writes an IEP outlining how the student will be helped. She also schedules a meeting so the IEP can be discussed with the student's parents. This requires lots of logistics as she, the parents, a classroom teacher, an administrator, and possibly the school psychologist must all attend the meeting. In addition, she has to have one meeting every year with the parents of all of her students to discuss and possibly modify each student's IEP. Sandi also has to work closely with an assistant who goes into the regular classrooms to help students in her resource classes. Some of her time is devoted to working with the mainstream classroom teachers on ways to help the special education students in their classes. Plus, there is all the record keeping for her classroom as well as the task of investigating and deciding whether students that were recommended by teachers, counselors, and parents need to be evaluated for learning disabilities.

Being a resource teacher allows Sandi to work with other teachers. She believes that many classroom teachers feel isolated as they don't have much opportunity to interact with their peers. In addition, she likes the variety teaching and assessment offer.

Working as a Special Education Teacher

JoAnn Finch-Martin teaches K–2 children in a classroom in a public school. She has a degree in education with a special education endorsement. JoAnn's job is challenging because her eight students have multiple disabilities, and lesson plans must be individualized for the special needs of each of them. Because her students have such profound handicaps as autism, Down's syndrome, cerebral palsy, and moderate mental retardation, she has two classroom aides. The students will spend the entire day from 8:40 A.M. to 3:40 P.M. in her classroom except for thirty minutes in the afternoon, when they are included in a regular first grade class for instruction in art, music, or physical education.

JoAnn's day begins when she assists four of her students eat breakfast in the school cafeteria. She helps two of them open their eating utensils and food packs and explains that learning to handle this task is part of the students' formal goals—acquisition of fine motor manipulation skills. Breakfast lasts only for about twenty-four minutes, but it is a hectic time with JoAnn always on her feet helping the four students.

The day continues in the classroom where the students hang up their coats, take down the chairs, and then go to the rest room to wash their faces and hands and take care of any other toileting needs. JoAnn has tried to design the curriculum so that her students' activities are similar to those in the regular classroom setting. The daily routine begins with the saying of the Pledge of Allegiance, followed by the morning circle. During this time, the students participate in a variety of activities from calendar reading and counting the days on the calendar to drilling on colors, shapes, and the alphabet. Both JoAnn and the aides encourage the children for the slightest participation.

After morning circle, the students take a quick rest room break. Two of the children have goals to improve their toileting skills, which require the attention of JoAnn and the aides. During the snack break that follows, all of the children are helped to work on their eating goals. After snack time, the children clean the table, push the chairs in, and sweep the floor. Then they join together on the carpet to do their morning exercises, which are followed by time at the gadget center. There the children work on such tasks as sorting colors and making chains from links. The morning ends with the children choosing a special activity. Although this time is called recreation and leisure time, there is really no leisure for JoAnn and her aids, as each child needs constant individual attention.

Lunch is a repeat of breakfast, with the students requiring the active assistance of JoAnn and the aides. It is followed by recess and a rest room break. Then there is a downtime with dim lights, music, and low activity for these medically fragile children. This is followed by a thirty-minute period in which the children are included in the activities of a regular classroom. The aides accompany the students while JoAnn uses the time as a preparation period. When the students return to the classroom, they engage in large-group activities such as coloring or letter bingo for the rest of the day. Some days they will take excursions into the community.

ENGLISH AS A SECOND LANGUAGE AND BILINGUAL TEACHERS

Immigrants have to speak English in order to function successfully in the United States. Until the 1960s, young immigrants entered school and were in a "sink or swim" situation in which they typically had to learn English without any special instruction. It wasn't until the wave of Cuban immigrants entered Florida in the 1960s that bilingual classes really began to emerge. Legislation was soon passed to allow students to receive instruction in their first language until they were ready to make the transition to English-only classes, usually by fourth grade. Besides bilingual programs, there are English as a Second Language (ESL) programs that let non-English speaking children spend most of their time in the regular classroom. In these programs, the children receive special help to learn English either in their regular classroom or in a special classroom for part of the day. The instruction is in English.

Job Requirements

Most ESL and bilingual instruction is at the elementary school level, which requires these teachers to hold elementary certification. They also need special certification. Bilingual teachers have to be proficient in the language of their students and thoroughly familiar with their culture. ESL teachers will teach children who speak many different languages, so they do not have to speak all of them. Obviously, it is very helpful if they are familiar with the languages and cultures of the students whom they will be teaching.

Job Opportunities

Since the number of non-English speaking students has grown dramatically in recent years, especially in California and Florida, there is a strong demand for bilingual and ESL teachers. You must remember that this is a very small number of the entire population of teachers. While most bilingual and ESL teachers work at the elementary level, a few are employed at the middle school and high school levels. In addition, there is a need for ESL teachers for adult education classes and special classes for immigrants. Most of these jobs will be part-time.

Working as an ESL Teacher

It is very important to understand that there is tremendous variety in the way ESL programs are set up in different states and even within different school districts in a state. Carol Bell is an ESL teacher who teaches classes in both middle school and senior high school and works with teachers and aides in an elementary school ESL program. She is an experienced teacher who began her career by teaching English to Central African students while serving in the Peace Corps. She also has taught in college language programs and tutored ESL students. Carol holds the appropriate credentials for this career: a bachelor's degree in high school English and certification as an ESL teacher. Although ESL instruction in her classes is given in English, it is a decided career plus that she has knowledge of French.

Because the number of ESL students in the district where Carol works is not large, she must move between schools. Her day begins at a middle school, where she teaches a class of fourteen students with beginning to advanced English language skills. This class, like all of her classes, is composed of students with a variety of first languages: German, Chinese, Spanish, Russian, Portuguese, and Yugoslavian. In this class, Carol designs a curriculum that focuses on helping her students read and write English and build their vocabularies. She uses a great number of strategies including direct teaching, acting out stories, class discussions, and having the students work in groups and pairs.

After her class at the middle school, Carol moves to an elementary school. Her role here is to assist the aides and teachers in finding instructional materials and developing skills in ESL teaching. At the school, she also does some testing of ESL students to determine their ability to handle English. Carol leaves the elementary school after two hours to spend the rest of the day at the high school, where she teaches a beginning and an advanced ESL class.

An extraordinary thing happens at the high school where she eats lunch every day with her students. They greet her with hugs and eagerly talk to her about their day. She is their support system in a challenging world where their language skills are limited, it's difficult to make friends, and the culture is not a familiar one. Because Carol's class is so important and appreciated by her students, many of them keep in touch with her after they leave high school to tell her how they are doing. In the beginning class, Carol tries to help the students become good readers and writers as soon as possible, while in the advanced class emphasis is placed on writing complete essays and developing a more sophisticated vocabulary for college admissions tests.

Teaching in ESL programs lets Carol have smaller classes. It also gives her the opportunity to meet students from other cultures and to watch them bloom. At the same time, it involves considerable preparation as there are insufficient adopted materials to meet her students' needs.

WORKING IN GIFTED AND TALENTED PROGRAMS

Although there are many programs in elementary, middle, and high school for gifted and talented students, few of these programs offer full-time jobs. Most teachers of the gifted and talented are also classroom teachers. For these positions, many states mandate that teachers have certification in this area or at least one or more courses. There are some full-time positions for individuals as district, county, and state coordinators of gifted and talented programs. These positions may require individuals to have master's degrees in gifted and talented education. Also, at the college level, summer programs for the gifted and talented require full-time teachers. Applicants for these positions should have experience in working with gifted and talented students and/or course work in this area. The directors of these programs often work throughout the year in the development of these programs. There are also college teachers who teach courses on gifted and talented education.

FOR MORE INFORMATION

To find out more about a career as a special education teacher, read *Opportunities in Special Education Careers,* published by VGM Career Horizons, and contact:

National Clearinghouse for Professions in Special Education
    Council for Exceptional Children
    1920 Association Drive
    Reston, VA 20191
    Web site: www.cec.sped.org

For more information about working as a bilingual teacher, read *Teaching English to Speakers of Other Languages,* published by VGM Career Horizons, and contact:

National Association for Bilingual Education
    Union Center Plaza, 39th Floor
    810 First Street NE
    Washington, DC 20002

To learn more about teaching English as a second language, read the previously mentioned book, and contact:

Association of Teachers of English as a Second Language
    National Association for Foreign Student Affairs (NAFSA)
    1860 Nineteenth Street NW
    Washington, DC 20009

CHAPTER 4

JOBS IN ADVISING AND COUNSELING STUDENTS

Although teachers hold most jobs in elementary, middle, junior, and senior high schools, counselors, deans, psychologists, and nurses also play very important, but different, roles in educating students. They smooth the educational path for those who are having problems from academic difficulties to health issues. Just as parents provide a support network at home, these professionals are students' support network at school—always ready to talk about problems and to answer questions.

COUNSELORS

School counselors help students understand and deal with their academic, career, social, behavioral, and personal problems. They are there for students who are being bullied by other students, failing a math class, or worrying about finding the right college or career. Another part of their job is to assist students in evaluating their interests and abilities.

Counselors don't just work with students when they have problems; they are also information providers who have solid knowledge about special programs for the gifted and learning disabled, about college and career entrance requirements, and about financial aid for colleges. Many counselors provide special services, such as alcohol and drug prevention programs and conflict resolution classes. Counselors also try to identify cases involving domestic abuse and other family problems that can affect a student's development.

In handling their job, counselors employ preventive and developmental counseling so that their students have the life skills necessary to deal with problems before they occur. They use interviews, counseling sessions, tests, or other methods when evaluating and advising students. Counselors work with students individually, in small groups, or in entire classes. They also consult and work with parents, teachers, school administrators, school psychologists, school nurses, and social workers.

A typical day for counselors is always busy and their offices are rarely empty; today, some counselors support as many as six hundred students. Most school counselors will work nine or ten months a year; however, this will vary in year-round schools and in schools supporting summer sessions. School counselors generally have the same hours as teachers. In order to keep their discussions private—an element essential to counseling—most counselors have private offices.

Elementary and Middle School Counselors

At the elementary and middle school levels, counselors are primarily involved with social and personal counseling. They observe children playing and working in the classroom and take particular note of children's interactions with other children and adults. They also confer with the children and their teachers and parents to evaluate the children's strengths, problems, and special needs. In addition, counselors help children develop good study habits and improve their organizational skills.

Junior and Senior High School Counselors

At the junior and senior high school levels, counselors help students evaluate their abilities, interests, talents, and personality characteristics so that the students can develop realistic academic and career goals. A large part of their job is helping students select appropriate and challenging classes to prepare for college or a career after completing high school. Counselors also provide information on all facets of selecting the right college and being admitted to it and on trade and technical schools and apprenticeship programs. At some schools, counselors have distinct responsibilities, with some spending all of their time doing career and/or college counseling while others work with students on course selection and any problems they may have.

Education Requirements

A counselor is expected to help students understand and resolve both academic and social problems. Therefore, it is essential for counselors to be well trained in multiple methods of communication and evaluation. The majority of school counselors will hold master's degrees in elementary or secondary school counseling, education, counseling psychology, or a related field. Graduate-level counselor education programs in colleges and universities usually are in departments of education or psychology. Within these departments, courses are generally grouped into eight core areas: human growth and development, social and cultural foundations, helping relationships, groups, lifestyle and career development, appraisal, research and evaluation, and professional orientation. In order to receive a master's degree from an accredited program, you will need forty-eight to sixty semester hours of graduate study including a period of supervised clinical experience.

Certification and Licensing

Although school counselors are required to hold state school counseling certification no matter what state they reside in, the certification requirements will vary from state to state. Some states require public school counselors to have both counseling and teaching certificates, while others may require a master's degree in counseling and two to five years of teaching experience.

Today, many counselors make the decision to earn the highly respected general practice credential of "National Certified Counselor." To become nationally certified by the National Board for Certified Counselors (NBCC), a counselor must hold a master's degree in counseling from a regionally accredited institution, have at least two years of supervised professional counseling experience, and pass NBCC's National Counselor Examination for Licensure and Certification. Although the NBCC certification is time consuming and rigorous, many states will accept this certification in lieu of their own state certification examination. Counselors who are NBCC certified will need to complete one hundred hours of continuing education credit every five years in order to maintain their certification status.

Special Attributes Needed

Counselors must like to work with and help others and should be able to work independently or as part of a team. They need to have the ability to inspire respect, trust, and confidence. In addition, counselors must possess high levels of physical and emotional energy in order to handle the wide array of problems they address. Unfortunately, dealing with these day-to-day problems can cause stress and emotional burnout.

Salaries and Fringe Benefits

Just like teachers' salaries, counselors' salaries will depend upon their level of education, work experience, job location, and employer. The average salary of public school counselors exceeds $44,000 per year. Many school counselors are compensated on the same pay scale as teachers. Some are able to earn additional income working in the summer in their school systems or in other jobs. The benefit plans for counselors are similar to those offered to teachers and generally include paid vacation; sick leave; medical, dental, and vision health care plans; life insurance; and retirement plans.

Career Path

As elementary, middle, and high school counselors gain work experience and continue to meet their ongoing education requirements, they may advance. Counselors with graduate course work can go on to positions such as head counselor, director of pupil services, director of guidance, or dean. In colleges and universities, counselors with advanced degrees can become deans of students, deans of placement or personnel services, financial aid directors, or even supervisors of testing. Some counselors may elect to work at a state department of education.

Working as a Counselor

Nancy Reagan is a very busy guidance counselor at a high school in southern Florida. She is responsible for about 450 students, a relatively small load when compared to the more than 600 students some counselors have. Nancy works in a small guidance office with a computer terminal operator, a guidance secretary, and a middle school counselor. Their immediate administrative supervisor is the Assistant Principal for Curriculum. The office is usually full of activity with students coming and going. Staff members are very friendly and helpful and obviously enjoy working with people. They are flexible and able to diffuse situations, such as dealing with angry parents, as they occur. Nancy's working hours tend to be dictated by parent or staff meetings in the mornings and afternoons. However, she usually arrives an hour or so before the students and leaves approximately one hour after the school day ends.

As a counselor, Nancy works with teachers, administrators, parents, and students. She frequently meets with students on an individual basis to talk over personal or academic concerns. Although most of these meetings are initiated by students, some may be the result of a referral from concerned parents, teachers, or peers. Her job as counselor is definitely not a simple one, as it also entails the following responsibilities:

- As the head of the guidance department, Nancy reports to the administration on student and curriculum concerns, pupil attendance, standardized testing, scheduling, and other departmental matters.
- Nancy also is frequently called upon to run parent-teacher conferences to monitor the progress of a student.
- At times, Nancy serves as a mediator in conflict situations involving students and occasionally mediates situations involving students and teachers.
- Nancy is the coordinator for Exceptional Student Education, a position that involves monitoring the meetings, completing legal paperwork, and administering individualized achievement tests.

- Nancy is also in charge of running student support groups on topics ranging from self-esteem to grief, family problems, and addiction issues.
- She is responsible for class schedules for each senior high school student and tracks his or her progress toward graduation, postsecondary education, and finding scholarships.

In addition to the above responsibilities, Nancy takes the time to make herself available for classroom presentations on goal setting and decision making, study skills, time management, stress management, conflict resolution, career planning, and wellness, which includes drug, alcohol, and sex education topics. She even provides parent in-service programs on postsecondary planning for their children as well as on the college application process and college financing.

NANCY'S EDUCATION

If you want to become a guidance counselor, you will need to obtain a master's degree in guidance. At the graduate level, Nancy's training included assessment and interpretation, counseling theories and practices, and career counseling courses. She also learned to do consultation with other professionals and run groups. Now that she is working as a counselor, Nancy's ongoing training has been more focused on the paperwork and technology required by the county and state. Counselors in her county meet several times during the year to update one another on changes in graduation requirements, scholarship requirements, standardized testing, and other guidance related concerns.

CAREER PATH

Before becoming a guidance counselor, Nancy worked as a classroom teacher for ten years. She taught students in special education and was trained to be a peer facilitator. When the funding for her peer program was cut, she began her training in guidance. Nancy is so happy in her current job as a guidance counselor that she has no immediate plans to leave this career. At some point in the future, she may try to move to a position in student services at the college level. She also would like to teach counselors in training but currently has no desire to pursue a doctorate.

CAREER PLUSES AND MINUSES

Nancy gets the greatest pleasure from her job when she works with students individually. She finds it very rewarding to develop relationships of mutual respect with young people and to provide them with support and guidance in their decision making. Nancy's goal is to empower her students so they can make mature decisions and take responsibility for the consequences of their choices. One of the most enjoyable aspects of her job is getting to see students mature from struggling adolescents to responsible young adults who are very proud of themselves and their accomplishments.

The downside to Nancy's job is having to deal with angry people. Parents are very passionate about their children and may not agree with her suggestions concerning their children. Nancy finds it to be very difficult not to take their anger personally. It is also difficult to have students get upset with her for being "on their case." Nancy believes that you have to learn to care enough to stay strong in your commitment to doing what is best for a child, even when it would be easier to give up or give in. She points out that you also have to know when to admit you are wrong and apologize.

Working as a counselor can be very stressful. There is a lot of pressure in handling deadlines and scheduling. One mistake by her could alter a student's graduation plans or scholarship possibilities. In addition, any inadvertent errors in the administration and supervision of standardized testing could result in invalidation and investigation on the county and state levels.

Nancy strongly recommends anyone interested in counseling spend at least three years in the classroom, because teaching gives insights into the concerns of parents and other adults working with students. This insight is critical to developing an empathetic attitude when running parent-teacher conferences or presenting other points of view to a student. She also believes that it is critical to stay current on adolescent issues and suggests that future counselors get as much training as possible in drugs, gangs, suicide prevention, depression, pregnancy, and other serious issues. Her final recommendation for counselors is to keep themselves mentally healthy, as counselors are ineffective in helping others if they cannot deal with their own problems.

Job Opportunities

Because school enrollment is growing, the need for counselors, especially in high school, will increase. Plus, many states are passing legislation requiring counselors in elementary schools. This job growth may be dampened, however, by government budgetary constraints. When money is tight, schools typically hire more teachers to handle the increased head count rather than counselors.

For More Career Information

To learn more about being a counselor, talk to counselors who are working at schools. State departments of education can supply information on colleges and universities that offer approved guidance and counseling training for state certification and licensure requirements. State employment service offices have information about job opportunities and entrance requirements for counselors. In addition, each state will have an association for counseling and development and a commission on teacher credentialing.

For general information on counseling, write to:

American School Counselor Association
   801 North Fairfax Street, Suite 310
   Alexandria, VA 22314
   (800) 306-4722
   Web site: www.schoolcounselor.org

For information on accredited counseling and related training programs, contact:

Council for Accreditation of Counseling and Related Educational
      Programs
   American Counseling Association
   5999 Stevenson Avenue
   Alexandria, VA 22304

For information on national certification requirements for counselors, contact:

National Board for Certified Counselors
   3 Terrace Way, Suite D
   Greensboro, NC 27403
   Web site: www.nbcc.org

SCHOOL PSYCHOLOGISTS

Psychologists study the human mind and behavior. They have been trained to conduct research, teach, evaluate, counsel, and advise others. School psychologists work in elementary and secondary schools or school district offices. They work with students, teachers, parents, and administrators to resolve students' learning and behavior problems. This may involve individual counseling.

They often will do individual testing to identify gifted students and those with learning disabilities. In addition, they strive to find the proper educational placement for these students. They frequently are part of the team creating independent education plans for learning disabled students. School psychologists also collaborate with teachers to improve classroom management and teaching and learning strategies. In some school districts, the psychologists may evaluate the effectiveness of academic programs, behavior management procedures, and other services provided in the school setting.

Education and Certification Requirements

To become a school psychologist, you must meet demanding standards. You need to have a master's degree in psychology and have completed an internship. Unfortunately, there is a great deal of competition for admission into graduate programs. While some universities require an undergraduate major in psychology, others will accept basic course work in psychology combined with other scientific classes.

School psychologists must obtain certification or meet state licensing requirements. Similar to the counseling profession, licensing laws for school psychologists will vary by state and by type of position. In addition, all states require that applicants pass an examination. Most states give board examinations consisting of a standardized test followed by oral or essay questions.

Special Attributes

Aspiring school psychologists must be emotionally stable, mature, and able to deal effectively with people. Sensitivity, compassion, and the ability to lead and inspire others are particularly important qualities for counseling. It is essential that school psychologists possess excellent communications skills. It is equally important for them to have patience and perseverance, as results from the psychological treatment of patients may take a long time.

Job Opportunities and Salaries

Being a school psychologist is being part of a very small profession compared to teaching, and even counseling. School districts usually will not have more than one psychologist, and some small districts will share the services of a psychologist. Employment of psychologists should grow, however, as schools are expected to increase student counseling and mental health services.

According to a survey by the American Psychological Association, the average annual salary of school psychologists with master's degrees was $60,000. They will have similar benefits to other employees in school district offices.

For More Information

In order to obtain information on careers, educational requirements, financial assistance, and licensing in all fields of psychology, contact:

American Psychological Association
Research Office and Education in Psychology and Accreditation
Offices
750 First Street NE
Washington, DC 20002
Web site: www.apa.org

For information on careers, educational requirements, and licensing of school psychologists, contact:

National Association of School Psychologists
4030 East West Highway, Suite 402
Bethesda, MD 20814

You can obtain information about state licensing requirements from:

Association of State and Provincial Psychology Boards
P.O. Box 4389
Montgomery, AL 36103-4389

DEANS

Deans have the task of providing support and guidance to students. They also are frequently responsible for disciplining students who have failed to follow a school's rules. The larger a high school is, the greater the number of deans and the more specific their duties become. Some deans have virtually jack-of-all-trades jobs as they administer discipline and counsel students plus take on the added responsibilities of handling attendance, coordinating the activities of the athletics department, overseeing the counseling program, arranging events, overseeing student government, supervising grounds and cafeterias, and even designing and implementing a school's curriculum. It is also a certainty that deans will spend considerable time after school and in the evening supervising school events.

Before becoming deans, most have held teaching or counseling positions in which they were able to demonstrate an exceptional ability to work with and help young adults. They also have shown themselves to be capable teachers who can handle additional responsibilities.

Education Requirements

Most deans begin their careers in related occupations such as teachers or counselors and prepare for a job in education administration by completing a master's degree. To be a successful dean, knowledge of management principles and practices, gained through work experience and formal education, is important. In most but not all public middle and senior high schools, deans will need to have or be taking classes for a master's degree in education administration or educational supervision; requirements for licensure vary by state.

Salary

Most academic deans work more than forty hours per week and frequently put in weeknight and weekend hours overseeing school activities. Many deans will work ten or eleven months a year, while others work year-round. Deans typically earn more than teachers, yet significantly less than principals.

Working as a Dean

Caleb Johnson is currently working as the dean of students at a senior high school. In this job, Caleb is responsible for all aspects of student discipline and for the school's athletic programs. In his role as disciplinarian, Caleb tracks students' detentions, suspensions, and expulsions that have resulted from violation of school rules. The rules are developed by a school committee and by the county or state and include everything from dress code, parking lot, fighting, smoking, and drug violations.

While handling student discipline, Caleb is formal, stern, and unyielding. When a student is sent to his office for breaking one of the rules, Caleb sits him or her down in a chair directly across from his desk and asks for an explanation. Often, making direct eye contact with students and asking probing questions will make them uncomfortable, with any luck so uncomfortable, that they will not want to return to his office. When working with the athletics program, Caleb wears a different face. He is casual and jovial with students and coaches. It is his responsibility to support the school's coaches in more than ten different sports for boys and girls. He helps them schedule games and buses for transportation. He also acts as an intermediary between the school's coaches and the county board of athletics. Caleb attends virtually all of the sporting events and always wear his school's colors with pride.

ON THE JOB

Being responsible for both discipline and athletics gives Caleb many busy workdays at his school. He spends at least one hour each morning attending to those students who have failed to follow the dress code. The rest of his morning and early afternoon is spent in meetings with students, their parents, teachers, and occasionally even the principal. These meetings can get ugly when students or parents become irate over the course of action he has chosen. In between his meetings, Caleb must update the computer database with his disciplinary actions, draft letters to parents, work and meet with the coaches to discuss their concerns, schedule sporting events, and order equipment and uniforms. Caleb is very pleased to be working at his high school because he gets such tremendous support from his principal and the office staff.

CAREER PATH

Caleb worked as a physical education teacher for seven years before becoming the dean of students. He believes that working as a teacher gave him the invaluable knowledge on how to work with and manage young adults. In the future, Caleb would like to climb the career ladder to become an assistant principal and then finish his career in education as a principal.

Job Opportunities

Job opportunities for deans are expected to grow in the next few years. The increases are expected because of the growing numbers of students attending school and the corresponding number of new schools being built. At this time, fewer and fewer individuals are seeking positions as deans because the salary is not seen to be commensurate with the workload.

SCHOOL NURSES

School nurses are a fundamental element of support for all students in an academic environment. Not only do nurses treat students for injuries, they diagnose illnesses and determine if children can remain at school. Children also are able to confide their health problems to school nurses. The nurses' responsibilities include promoting the health and nutrition of all of the schoolchildren in their care. They may do this by establishing educational programs for students as well as their parents and through screening the children for health problems such as vision and hearing. Keeping medical records up to date is another part of their job. In recent years, as federal law has mandated the mainstreaming of many disabled children, school nurses have been given such new tasks as dispensing medicines and inserting catheters. In addition, many school nurses arrange for health care for children whose families cannot afford it.

According to the American Nursing Association, there are approximately thirty thousand school nurses. Many wear beepers and serve as many as ten elementary schools. In schools that do not have nurses, an aide or secretary often has the responsibility of handling sick or injured children.

Education and Training

In order to work in a school, you must be a registered nurse (R.N.). To become licensed, all states require students to graduate from a nursing program and pass a national licensing examination. Nurses may be licensed in more than one state, either by examination or endorsement of a license issued by another state. As with most certifications, nurses must periodically renew their licenses. Some states may require nurses to continue their education in order to renew their licenses.

There are three different educational paths you can take to become a registered nurse: A.D.N., B.S.N., and diploma. An A.D.N., or associate degree program, is typically offered by community and junior colleges and takes about two years to complete. Nearly two-thirds of all R.N. graduates come from A.D.N. programs. B.S.N., or bachelor's degree programs, are offered by colleges and universities and take anywhere from four to five years to complete. Close to one-third of all graduates are from these programs. The third and final way to become a nurse is through a diploma program given in hospitals that generally lasts two to three years. Only a very small number of graduates comes from these programs.

There have been and will continue to be attempts to raise the educational requirements for an R.N. license to a bachelor's degree. These changes, should they occur, will probably be made state by state, through legislation or regulation. Changes in licensure requirements would not affect currently licensed R.N.s, who would be "grandfathered." However, individuals considering nursing should carefully weigh the pros and cons of enrolling in a B.S.N. program, since their advancement opportunities are broader. In fact, some career paths are open only to nurses with bachelor's or advanced degrees.

Nursing education includes classroom instruction and supervised clinical experience in hospitals and other health facilities. Students take courses in anatomy, physiology, microbiology, chemistry, nutrition, psychology and other behavioral sciences, and nursing. Course work also includes liberal arts classes to ensure that the nurse is a well-rounded individual.

Special Attributes

In order to become a school nurse, an individual should be caring and sympathetic and able to accept responsibility. It is especially important for him or her to be able to determine when a doctor's consultation on a student is required. Plus, the nurse will need emotional stability in order to cope with emergencies and other stresses.

Job Opportunities and Salaries

Budget cuts have reduced the number of school nurses. However, communities have begun to insist that school districts employ more nurses. Recently, there has been a push for school-based clinics, which should increase the demand for school nurses. The average annual salary for full-time registered nurses is more than $33,000 a year.

For More Career Information

For a list of B.S.N. and graduate programs, write to:

American Association of Colleges of Nursing
1 Dupont Circle NW, Suite 530
Washington, DC 20036
Fax: (202) 785-8320

Another good source of information is the National League for Nursing (NLN). The NLN publishes a variety of nursing and nursing education materials, including a list of nursing programs and information on student financial aid. For a complete list of NLN publications, write for a career information brochure. Send your request to:

Communications Department
  National League for Nursing
  350 Hudson Street
  New York, NY 10014
  Fax: (212) 989-2272

Information on registered nurses also is available from:

American Nurses Association
  600 Maryland Avenue SW
  Washington, DC 20024-2571
  Web site: www.ana.org

CHAPTER 5

OPPORTUNITIES IN SCHOOL ADMINISTRATION

Competent administrators are required to ensure the smooth operation of an educational institution. Education administrators provide direction, leadership, and day-to-day management of educational activities in schools. Working with their school boards, they set educational standards and goals and establish the policies and procedures to carry them out.

The administrators in elementary, middle, and secondary schools are the principal and assistant principals. At the district level there are even more administrative positions. They include such positions as superintendents and assistant superintendents, curriculum directors, transportation directors, human resource directors, attendance directors, and building and grounds directors. These high-level administrative positions provide support to the individual schools ensuring that they have the resources they need. They also determine whether an individual school is maintaining an acceptable level of academic excellence.

PRINCIPALS

Principals are the school administrators that most people know. They are responsible for the management of elementary, middle, and secondary schools including the supervision of their support staff, teachers, counselors, librarians, coaches, and others. The size of the school dictates the number of administrators needed to ensure that it runs efficiently. In large schools, the multiple responsibilities are divided among many administrators, with each having a specific function. In a small school, one principal may handle all the administrative tasks.

Responsibilities

Principals determine the academic tone of the school. They hire teachers and other staff and help them to improve their skills while evaluating them to monitor their effectiveness. They visit classrooms, observe teaching methods, review instructional objectives, and examine learning materials. Principals work with their teachers to help them develop and maintain high curriculum standards, create personal and schoolwide mission statements, and set performance goals and objectives. It is essential that principals use clear and objective guidelines for teacher appraisals since pay is often based on performance ratings. Most principals meet with members of their staff on a weekly, if not daily basis, to offer advice and explanations or to answer procedural questions.

An important part of a principal's job is meeting and interacting with other administrators, students, parents, and representatives of community organizations. In the past decade, decision-making authority has shifted from school district central offices to individual schools. As a result, parents, teachers, and other members of the community are now playing an important role in setting school policies and goals. Principals must pay attention to the concerns of these groups when making administrative decisions.

Handling a school's finances is another vital aspect of this job. Principals are responsible for the creation of budgets and reports on various subjects, including finances and attendance. They also must request and allocate supplies to their teachers and support staff. As school budgets become tighter, many principals have become involved in public relations and fund-raising efforts to secure financial support for their schools from local businesses and the community. This is the only way some schools can have music and sports programs.

In today's schools, principals have to take an active role in ensuring their schools are on the right track to meeting the nation's academic standards. Many states now give schools public report cards based on the tested levels of achievement of their students. Schools that do not meet certain standards may be taken over and run by the state.

Schools are involved not only with the academic achievement of their students but also their emotional development. As a result, principals face responsibilities outside the academic realm. For example, in response to the growing number of dual-income and single-parent families and teenage parents, many principals have established before and after school child-care programs or family resource centers. These centers may even offer parenting classes and social service referrals. With the help of community organizations, some principals have established programs to combat the increase in crime, drug and alcohol abuse, and sexually transmitted disease among students.

Working as a Principal

Harold Maready is principal of a charter school that he started from the ground up in an effort to improve education. This combination junior/senior high school is a school of choice that students elect to attend for its distinctive offerings. What is so special about the school is how closely its educational goals are tied to the business world. It readies the students to enter the workforce. For example, the students actually run their own printing shop, which sells products to local companies, and an engineering group both designs and then builds the designs. Plus, all of the students have the opportunity to career shadow an employee in a local business twice a year, and seniors have semester-long internships with local businesses.

Harold is truly a pioneer in the development of this type of school. He obtained money from government grants and local businesses to start the school. Now, on a daily basis, he works to maintain the school's partner relationships with local businesses, parents, and other members of the community. Because of his school's unique composition, Harold is responsible for managing his own school budget—not the county. As a result, he and his business manager spend hours allotting money to various school activities and requesting money from local businesses and government grants.

A key factor in the school is Harold's leadership. He challenges and encourages his students to be successful by creating an environment that is creative and supportive. His style of leadership and the style he requires of his teachers, places a great deal of emphasis on team-building skills. Harold believes that these skills enable students to become positive members of society. He knows nearly all of his students by name and spends time in class and on campus with them on a daily basis. In a way, he even acts as a guidance counselor as he calls students to his office individually and in small groups to discuss their progress and get input on how they feel about the school. In addition to regular conferences and meetings, Harold provides parents with workshops and training to help them deal with difficult situations that may arise as their children mature.

Harold is frequently the first and last person at the school each day. He works such long hours because he spends so much of his schoolday with the students. Harold also holds weekly meetings for his leadership staff and monthly schoolwide meetings to ensure that his teachers are aware of the school's actions and that all have the opportunity to voice their opinions—both positive and negative.

CAREER PATH

Harold started his climb up the ladder to become principal in the traditional way by working as a teacher. After spending six years as an elementary and secondary school teacher, he worked briefly as an education consultant. When he returned to the school environment, he became principal at a school for children with learning disabilities and then principal at a vocational school. For part of this time, he also worked as an adjunct professor at a local university. His next career step was to establish his charter school. In the future, Harold plans to become a consultant for charter schools. He would like to visit school districts across the nation to teach them how they, too, can manage their own schools and make them more successful.

THE PLUSES AND MINUSES

Harold finds it gratifying to see the transformation in students who enter his school and become eager learners because of the school's dynamic program. Graduation never fails to bring tears to his eyes as he sees his students are truly prepared to become successful members of society. Harold also finds the relationships he develops with all types of students and the friendships he makes with his staff to be very rewarding. He loves working with, talking to, and helping people. The downsides to his job are the number of hours he has to put in to keep his school successful, and the occasional irate parent conference.

ASSISTANT PRINCIPALS

Assistant principals aid the principal in the overall administration of the school. Smaller schools, especially elementary schools, may not have assistant principals. Both junior and senior high schools tend to have assistant principals. Their responsibilities include determining which classes the school will offer, ordering textbooks and supplies, and coordinating transportation, custodial, cafeteria, and other support services. Assistant principals usually handle discipline, attendance, social and recreational programs, and health and safety. They also may counsel students on personal, educational, or vocational matters.

In the future, with site-based management, assistant principals will be expected to take on new roles; they will have to be team managers and have knowledge of public relations. As a result, they will need to possess the skills of group communication and shared decision-making. One way for them to attain these skills is through in-service education, although they also can attend leadership academies or other continuing education classes.

ADMINISTRATORS AT THE DISTRICT LEVEL

Administrators in school district central offices manage public schools under their jurisdiction. How large these offices are depends on the size of the district. Some may have hundreds of employees with very specific jobs, while others have just a handful who do several jobs. These administrators include people who direct subject-area programs such as English, music, vocational education, special education, and mathematics. They also include those responsible for planning, standardizing, evaluating, and improving curriculums and teaching techniques. Other administrators are directors of programs such as guidance, school psychology, athletics, curriculum and instruction, tests and measurement, and professional development. Plus, there are administrators who have the task of helping teachers improve their skills and learn about new methods and materials. And there are others who are responsible for the creation and maintenance of career counseling programs. They conduct and help create tests that measure students' abilities and help place them in appropriate classes.

SUPERINTENDENTS

Superintendents coordinate all the administrative responsibilities of the district, which include: business, finance, personnel, technological services, instructional services, transportation, vocational education, adult education, community education, and facilities and operations. They are considered to be general managers or top executives due to the number and complexity of the departments that they oversee. These administrators are responsible for implementing programs that further their policies within budgetary constraints and for creating strategies to ensure that their organizations' objectives are met.

Superintendents must have highly developed personal skills and analytical minds able to quickly assess large amounts of information and data. They must be able to evaluate the interrelationships of numerous factors, and they must be able to communicate clearly and persuasively.

The educational background of superintendents varies as widely as the nature of their responsibilities. School superintendents generally have an advanced degree, often a master's degree in education administration. A few have doctorates. Superintendents can be among the highest-paid workers in the nation, but long hours and substantial travel are often required.

ADMINISTRATIVE ORGANIZATIONAL CHART

By studying the organizational chart, you can easily see the number of administrators who are required to run a large school district. It is the elected board of education that has the ultimate responsibility for the education of the children in a school district, and the superintendent who carries out the wishes of the board with the assistance of the staff.

Working as an Administrator in Several Positions

The career path of Annette Saint Clair from kindergarten teacher to director of curriculum exemplifies how being prepared to do many jobs can give you a great number of options in education. After receiving her bachelor's degree in elementary education along with a K–12 teaching license, Annette began immediately to work on her master's degree. By taking no electives, she was able to receive a master's degrees in three areas—administration and supervision, director of guidance, and elementary education—as well as licensing. Her education did not end at this point. Instead, throughout her career, she has continued to take courses to expand her horizons and build skills in such areas as economics, curriculum, group counseling, diagnostic reading, and geography.

GUIDANCE COUNSELOR

While working in her first job as a kindergarten teacher, Annette also had been taking classes in guidance. In addition, she had demonstrated to the administration that she was a very successful teacher with outstanding organizational skills. When a new junior high school opened in the district, the superintendent noted that Annette had certification as a counselor and asked if she would be interested in being a guidance counselor. At first, she worked as a

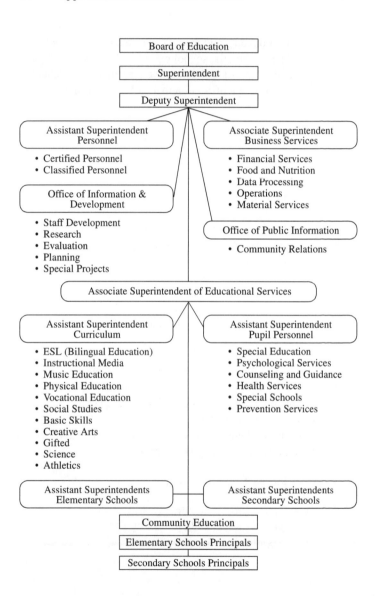

counselor for half the day, and the rest as a social studies and language arts teacher. When the school grew, she became a full-time counselor and director of guidance. At that time, the school's administration consisted of a principal, assistant principal, and director of guidance.

DIRECTOR OF GUIDANCE

A move to a new city and larger junior high school resulted in Annette working as a full-time guidance counselor. When the district opened a new junior high school, she remained at the school as director of guidance, directing the efforts of two and later on three other counselors. Annette had an extended weeks contract at this school, which meant that she worked a few weeks before and after the regular school year. Her responsibilities included counseling one-third of the students in grades six through nine. She would meet once a year with her students in grades seven, eight, and nine and their parents to plan the students' classes for the next year. The younger students were scheduled by class. After the students had selected their classes, it was her task to make the schedule for the school year. This was an immense undertaking for a school of more than one thousand students as computers were not then being used for scheduling. While serving as the director of guidance, Annette not only continued to take classes, but also wrote a grant that brought the school funds to establish a career center in the library, held the school's first career day, and established a sustained silent reading program for the entire school.

PRINCIPAL

Throughout her career, Annette has had mentors who have always challenged her to be ready to take on new responsibilities. While serving as director of guidance, she had worked on the plans for a new elementary school in the district. One of the people with whom she had done much team planning suggested that she apply for a position as principal. Annette applied and became the first female principal in the school district.

At this elementary school for more than six hundred students, Annette's only administrative help was the school secretary. This was a twelve-month job in which she supervised the staff, scheduled all students, and served as guidance counselor. At the same time, she was very active in local groups of the Association of School Principals and became the state president of the International Reading Association.

DIRECTOR OF ELEMENTARY EDUCATION

The administration of the school district noticed Annette's superior handling of her job, her participation in professional organizations, and her continuing efforts to learn even more about education through seminars and classes. The superintendent asked Annette to apply for the position of Director of Elementary Education as the present director was retiring.

Annette's major responsibility in this new position was focused on developing a strong curriculum for every subject in grades K–5 with the help of the teachers. Considerable time had to be spent each year in adopting textbooks. Committees had to be set up to handle the adoption process, which included a lot of research. Then, once new books were adopted, the program had to be implemented and evaluated. Other administrative responsibilities included advising on teacher hiring, visiting classrooms, coordinating the elementary curriculum with the junior and senior high school director, and serving as a representative on state department of education committees. At this time, the other administrators in the district were the superintendent, assistant superintendent, business manager, and a media services coordinator.

DIRECTOR OF CURRICULUM

A budget crunch, the resignation of the Director of Secondary Education, and the advent of a new superintendent resulted in the reorganization of the district administration staff. Annette became the Director of Curriculum for both the elementary and secondary school programs. Not only did she have all her former responsibilities, she now had to oversee the junior and senior high curriculums. The major task at the secondary level was to update the curriculum guides for each department.

One year later in this rapidly growing district, Annette's duties as Director of Curriculum were again changed as another curriculum director was hired. Now she was to oversee the K–12 language arts, social studies, and fine arts curriculums while the other director would be in charge of the K–12 mathematics, science, applied arts, and physical education programs. In addition, she would serve as the director of the elementary school principals; supervise the district's before and after school programs; and coordinate the guidance, special education, and gifted and talented programs. One of her first innovations in this position was to establish a new teachers' academy, which would meet monthly to help them improve their classroom management skills. Other administrators in the district included the superintendent, two assistant superintendents (one for business affairs and one for human resources), and directors of curriculum (2), human resources, and transportation to make a total of seven on the staff.

CAREER ADVICE

Annette strongly advises those who are just starting their careers to do as she has done and acquire a background in education that will give you numerous options. Teachers should strive to have more than one license. Then when a new opportunity emerges they will be ready to step in and advance their careers.

Education and Training Requirements

Most education administrators begin their careers in related occupations and prepare for a job in education administration by completing a master's or doctoral degree. Because there are so many different occupations, duties, and levels of responsibility within a school district, administrators can have diverse educational backgrounds and experiences.

Principals and assistant principals in public schools and administrators in central offices usually need to earn a master's degree in education administration or educational supervision. Some principals and central office administrators have a doctorate or specialized degree in education administration. In addition, virtually all states require principals to be licensed as school administrators. Requirements for licensure will vary by state.

National standards for school leaders, including principals and supervisors, were recently developed by the Interstate School Leaders Licensure Consortium. States may use these national standards as guidelines for licensure requirements or for activities such as mentoring, professional development, or accreditation of training programs. In private schools, which are not subject to state certification requirements, some principals and assistant principals hold only a bachelor's degree; however, the majority have a master's or doctoral degree.

Principals, assistant principals, and central office administrators have usually held teaching positions at some time before moving into administration. Some teachers move directly into principal positions, while others first become assistant principals. Teachers also can gain experience in other central office administrative jobs at either the school or district level as department heads, curriculum specialists, or subject matter advisors before becoming principals. Just as teaching is frequently the stepping-stone to jobs as principals, being a principal frequently leads to an administrative position in the central district office.

Attributes

In order to be considered for administrative positions, educators first must prove themselves in their current jobs. Just as in other professional careers, determination, confidence, innovativeness, motivation, and leadership are essential. Managerial attributes, such as the ability to make sound decisions and organize and coordinate work efficiently, are also very important. Since much of the job of administrators involves interacting with others—from students to parents to teachers—they must have strong interpersonal skills, be effective communicators, and be motivators.

Salaries

Salaries of education administrators vary according to position, level of responsibility, and experience; they also depend upon the size and location of the institution. Just as teachers employed in public schools generally earn higher salaries than those in private schools, it is the same story with principals.

According to a survey of public schools, conducted by the Educational Research Service, recent average salaries for principals and assistant principals were as follows:

Principals:
Elementary School	$62,900
Junior High/Middle School	66,900
Senior High School	72,400

Assistant Principals:
Elementary School	$52,300
Junior High/Middle School	56,500
Senior High School	59,700
Directors, Managers, Coordinators, and Supervisors of Instructional Services	70,800

Most education administrators work more than forty hours a week, including many nights and weekends when they oversee school activities. Many administrators work ten or eleven months a year. It is, however, becoming increasingly common for administrators to work all year due to the increased popularity of year-round schooling.

Fringe Benefits

Administrators may receive everything from money for professional development and continuing education to health care insurance as fringe benefits. Although not all school districts can afford to pay for their professionals' on-going education, most will pay at least part of the expenses incurred when traveling to professional meetings and conventions. Generally, the insurance benefits are comparable to if not better than those granted to teachers.

In addition, administrators also are entitled to retirement programs in which the state and federal government will match a percentage of the money deposited by the employee. Administrators can receive severance pay, an important aspect of the benefits as they are not able to receive tenure like teachers. Finally, administrators are able to take part in leave provisions. The amount and type of leave policies are determined by the local school system but typically include: vacation, sick, family, personal, jury, bereavement, military, religious, and sabbatical.

Job Opportunities

Education administrators hold close to four hundred thousand jobs. Almost nine out of ten jobs are in elementary, secondary, and technical schools and colleges and universities. The rest work in child day care centers, religious organizations, job training centers, state departments of education, and businesses and other organizations that provide training for their employees.

School enrollments at the elementary, secondary, and post-secondary levels are all expected to increase over the next decade. Rather than opening new schools, budget constraints will force many existing school populations to expand, thus increasing the demand for assistant principals to help with the increased work-load. Employment of education administrators also will grow as more services are provided to students and as efforts to improve the quality of education continue.

Competition will be keen for prestigious jobs in higher educa-tion, but it will be much less intense for jobs at the elementary and secondary school levels. It is becoming more difficult to attract candidates for principal, vice principal, and administration jobs because the pay is not significantly higher than teachers' and does not compensate for the added workload and responsibility of the position. In addition, teachers have recently been given more decision-making responsibilities, and site-based management is lessening their desire to move into administrative positions.

FOR MORE INFORMATION

For more information on elementary and secondary school prin-cipals, assistant principals, and central office administrators, con-tact one of the following:

American Federation of School Administrators
1729 Twenty-first Street NW
Washington, DC 20009

American Association of School Administrators
1801 North Moore Street
Arlington, VA 22209

For information on elementary school principals and assistant principals, contact:

National Association of Elementary School Principals
1615 Duke Street
Alexandria, VA 22314-3483

For information on secondary school principals and assistant principals, contact:

National Association of Secondary School Principals
1904 Association Drive
Reston, VA 20191

CHAPTER 6

JOBS AT COLLEGES AND UNIVERSITIES

There are more than three thousand colleges and universities in the United States, and each one of them offers many jobs in education. In fact, a large university will have a staff of more than ten thousand full- and part-time employees in the areas of administration, instruction, finance, health care, information, and student services. There are jobs for instructors teaching freshman English classes and full professors acting as department chairs. In development offices, a large staff is devoted to raising funds, while in alumni offices they are cementing schools' relationships with their graduates. Admissions officers are spending long hours reading hundreds of applications, and financial aid officers are juggling numbers to come up with aid packages for thousands of students. Careers in higher education are truly numerous and diverse.

ADMINISTRATORS IN HIGHER EDUCATION

College and university administrators supervise the operation of the school from the hiring of faculty members to the building of new residence halls. Each administrator has a staff assisting him or her in handling job responsibilities. Titles of positions available in college administration follow below. It is important to note that not all of the positions listed will be found in every college or university.

Administrative Positions:

Chief Business Officer
Chief Human Resources
   Officer
General Counsel
Director, Accounting
Director, Internal Audit
Director, Food Services
Director, Purchasing
Director, Campus Security
Director, Risk Management
Director, Affirmative Action

Chief Planning Officer
Chief Budgeting Officer
Director, Computer Center
Comptroller
Bursar
Facilities Management Officer
Director, Bookstore
Director, Auxiliary Services
Chief Planning and Budget Officer
Director, Housing and Food Service

External Affairs Positions:

Chief Development Officer
Director, Church Relations
Director, Information Services
Director, Alumni Affairs
Director, Community Services

Chief Public Relations Officer
Director, Special and Deferred Gifts
Director, News Bureau
Director, Information Office
Director, Publications

Student Affairs Positions:

Chaplain
Director, Student Activities
Director, Foreign Students
Director, Student Placement
Director, Student Health
   Services
Director, Student Housing

Dean of Students
Director, Admissions
Director, Student Financial Aid
Director, Student Counseling
Physical Administrator
Director, Athletics

Academic Positions:

President	Vice President
Chief Academic Officer, Provost	Chief Health Professions Officer
	Director, Learning Resource Center
Registrar	Director, Educational Media
Director, Library Services	Administrator, Grants and Contracts
Director, Institutional Research	Director, Admissions and Registrar
Director, International Studies	Dean, Agriculture
Dean, Architecture	Dean, Arts and Sciences
Dean, Arts and Letters	Dean, Communications
Dean, Business	Dean, Dentistry
Dean, Continuing Education	Dean, Engineering
Dean, Education	Dean, Graduate Programs
Dean, Fine Arts	Dean, Home Economics
Dean, Health Professions	Dean, Instruction
Dean, Humanities	Dean, Library and Information Services
Dean, Law	
Dean, Mathematics	Dean, Medicine
Dean, Music	Dean, Nursing
Dean, Occupational Studies	Dean, Pharmacy
Dean, Public Health	Dean, Sciences
Dean, Social Sciences	Dean, Social Work
Dean, Undergraduate Programs	Dean, Veterinary Medicine

It is relatively common for academic administrators, especially deans, to teach in addition to conducting their administrative duties as it helps them keep in touch with both their field of expertise and students. However, few top-level administrators such as presidents, vice presidents, and provosts spend any time in the classroom. Most of their time must be spent on management, public relations, and fund-raising duties. The more you know about the responsibilities of the different departments and offices at colleges and universities, the easier it will be for you to decide where you may wish to look for a position. A few administrative areas will be described for you in the next section.

Office of Academic Affairs

The office of academic affairs is dedicated to advancing the academic mission of the university. This office seeks to facilitate the learning, information retrieval, scholarship, and research of students, faculty, and staff on campus and in field-based and on-line programs. With a focus on learning, the office of academic affairs uses many techniques to support innovation, collaboration across multiple fields of study, and collegewide discussion and decision making.

Registrar's Office

The registrar's office is responsible for maintaining the academic records of all current and former students, including grades, majors, minors, degrees, and graduation honors received. The office tracks students' progress and is responsible for making sure that students have completed all of the requirements necessary to finish their degrees.

The registrar's office also assesses and collects tuition and fees, plans and implements commencement, oversees the preparation of college catalogs and schedules of classes, and analyzes enrollment and demographic statistics. It is important for registrars to have an understanding of and desire to use modern technology, especially web sites, because so much of the information they manage is available on-line for students, and this information must be constantly monitored and updated. The registrar's office also provides the following services:

academic standing
course evaluations
degree progress
end-quarter reports
examination scheduling
grading
major and minor declarations
courses and degrees (including the time schedule of classes and
    the course bulletin)
transfer credit and advanced placement
evaluation

Admissions Office

Directors of admissions manage the process of recruiting, evaluating, and admitting students. They are helped in this by assistant directors and admissions officers who read and evaluate applications. The hours will usually be very long for everyone in this office as the deadline for deciding on who to admit approaches each year. This is a department in which you can get a position after graduation from college and climb the career ladder to the top rung.

Student Activities

Directors of student activities staff plan and arrange social, cultural, and recreational activities on campus. They assist student-run organizations such as student government and cultural and academic clubs. Some even may be in charge of orienting new students to the school.

Athletic Department

Athletic directors, along with assistant athletic directors and staff, are responsible for planning and directing intercollegiate and intramural athletic activities, including publicity for athletic events, preparation of budgets, and supervision of coaches. Directors also are responsible for ensuring that their staff abides by the recruiting laws as established by the NCAA and athletic conferences in which the school competes.

Deans

In colleges and universities, academic deans, deans of faculty, provosts, and university deans assist college and university presidents in developing budgets and creating academic policies and programs. They also direct and coordinate activities for the heads of individual colleges and chairpersons of academic departments. And many take an active role in the classroom.

Education Requirements

In order to obtain a top administrative position in a college or university, you will need an advanced degree in higher education administration, educational supervision, or college student affairs. Education administration degree programs include courses in: school management, school law, school finance and budgeting, curriculum development and evaluation, research design and data analysis, community relations, politics in education, counseling, and leadership. Educational supervision degree programs include courses in supervision of instruction and curriculum, human relations, curriculum development, research, and advanced pedagogy courses. Academic deans and chairpersons usually have a doctorate in their specialty. Most have held a professorship before becoming administrators.

It is possible to start in entry-level jobs in admissions, student affairs, financial aid, and the registrar's office with bachelor's degrees and then advance to top administrative posts after earning doctoral degrees. For these entry-level jobs, computer literacy and a background in mathematics and statistics are definite assets.

Salaries

As schools grow in size so grow their need for administrators. Today, many colleges have an organizational structure very similar to those found in large businesses. Top school administrators, especially those working for large colleges and universities, are considered to be the equivalent of corporate America's CEO's. As a result, many members of the administration and faculty, especially those in the upper levels, have never been paid more. The following salary charts from the College and University Personnel Association reflect recent salaries of administrators in several areas.

Median Annual Salaries of Administrators

Title	Public Universities	Private Universities
Chancellor, System	$116,142	$120,000
President, Institution	103,000	140,000
Executive Vice President	92,299	122,175
Chief Academic Officer	85,500	90,000
Chief Business Officer	78,900	89,439
Chief Financial Officer	71,901	72,000
Chief Planning Officer	73,166	74,550
Chief Budgeting Officer	59,495	65,000
Chief Development Officer	72,500	82,800

Median Annual Salaries of Administrators (continued)

Title	Public Universities	Private Universities
Chief Public Relations Officer	53,334	57,601
Director of Alumni Affairs	44,714	41,700
Chief Student Affairs Officer	72,875	71,500
Chief Admissions Officer	51,169	55,639
Registrar	49,169	42,900
Director of Financial Aid	46,215	44,656
Director of Career Development and Placement	43,780	39,303
Director of Student Counseling	50,040	42,997

Median Annual Salaries of Academic Deans

Discipline	Salary
Medicine	$201,200
Law	141,400
Engineering	112,800
Arts and Sciences	82,500
Business	81,700
Mathematics	59,900
Social Sciences	61,800
Education	80,000

Median Annual Salaries of Student Services Directors

Discipline	Salary
Admissions and Registrar	$50,700
Student Financial Aid	45,400
Student Activities	34,500

Job Opportunities

In the immediate future, substantial competition is expected for those who seek prestigious jobs as higher education administrators. Many faculty and other staff meet the education and experience requirements for these jobs and seek promotion. Furthermore, the number of openings is relatively small, and only the most highly qualified are selected. It also must be noted that budget constraints could limit growth in this profession. A few colleges and universities have been reducing their administrative staffs to contain costs, while others are consolidating administrative jobs and contracting with other providers for some administrative functions. Candidates who have the most formal education and who are willing to relocate should have the best job prospects.

COLLEGE AND UNIVERSITY FACULTY

Today, college and university faculty teach and advise nearly fifteen million full- and part-time students. Not only do they teach in the classroom, they also may teach "satellite" courses that are broadcast to students at off-campus sites through closed-circuit or cable television. Some even teach courses on-line, where the classroom is located on the Internet. Increasingly, they find themselves working with a more varied population of part-time, older, and culturally and racially diverse students.

Faculty members generally work in a department or division, based on their subject or field, and teach several courses. For example, a professor in the foreign language department might teach courses in both Spanish literature and grammar while someone in the art department might teach painting and art history. Their teaching may involve giving lectures to several hundred students in large halls, leading small seminars and discussion groups, and supervising students in laboratory activities. They prepare lectures, exercises, and laboratory experiments; create tests; grade examinations and papers; and advise and work with students individually.

Additional Responsibilities

Faculty at universities also are responsible for counseling, advising, teaching, and supervising graduate students. In addition to their teaching duties, college and university faculty study and meet with colleagues, read professional journals, and participate in professional conferences to keep abreast of developments in their field. They are expected to spend time conducting research to expand knowledge in their field. The amount of time varies with the school; however, faculty at universities generally spend a significant part of their time doing research. In their research, they may conduct experiments, collect and analyze data, and examine original documents, literature, and other source material. From this they develop hypotheses, arrive at conclusions, and publish their findings in scholarly journals, books, and electronic media. Most faculty members serve on academic or administrative committees that deal with the policies of their institution, departmental matters, academic issues, curricula, budgets, equipment purchases, and hiring. Some also will work with student as well as community organizations.

On the Job

College faculty generally have flexible schedules. They must be present for classes, usually twelve to sixteen hours a week, and for faculty and committee meetings. Most establish regular office hours for student consultations, usually three to six hours per week. Otherwise, faculty are free to decide when and where they will work, and how much time to devote to course preparation, grading papers and exams, study, research, graduate student supervision, and other activities. Some faculty members work staggered hours and teach classes at night and on weekends. Most faculty are employed on a nine-month contract, which gives them the time to teach, do research, travel, or pursue nonacademic interests during the summer and school holidays.

Many colleges are increasing their reliance on part-time faculty, who generally have limited administrative and student advising duties, which leaves the declining number of full-time faculty with a heavier workload. Part-time faculty generally spend little time on campus, because they usually don't have an office. In addition, they may teach at more than one college, requiring travel between their various places of employment, earning the name "gypsy faculty." They are not usually eligible for tenure, and as a result their lack of job security can be stressful.

College and university faculty increasingly use technology in all areas of their work. In the classroom, they may use computers, including the Internet; electronic mail; software programs, such as statistical packages; and CD-ROMs as teaching aids. Faculty also use computers to do their own research, participate in discussion groups in their field, or publicize their professional research papers.

Department Heads

College and university department heads are in charge of an entire department such as history, English, or economics. In addition to teaching, they coordinate department schedules of classes and teaching assignments, propose budgets, and recruit, interview, and hire applicants for teaching positions. They also evaluate department faculty members, encourage their development, and perform other administrative duties. In overseeing their departments, department heads must consider and balance the concerns of faculty, administrators, and students.

Education Requirements

Full-time college and university professors almost always need to have a doctoral degree (Ph.D.). Doctoral programs, including time spent completing a master's degree and a dissertation, take an average of six to eight years of full-time study beyond the bachelor's degree. Some programs, such as the humanities, take longer to complete; others, such as engineering are generally shorter. Degree candidates specialize in a subfield of a discipline, such as organic chemistry or European history. At the same time, they usually take courses covering the entire discipline. Programs include twenty or more increasingly specialized courses and seminars in addition to comprehensive examinations on all major areas of the field.

In addition to the course work, doctoral degree candidates also must complete a dissertation—a written report on original research in their field of study. The dissertation sets forth an original hypothesis or proposes a model and tests it. Students in the natural sciences and engineering usually do laboratory work, while in the humanities, they study original documents and other published material. The dissertation, done under the guidance of one or more faculty advisors, usually takes one or two years of full-time work.

In some fields, particularly the natural sciences, some Ph.D. holders spend an additional two years on postdoctoral research and study before taking a faculty position. They may extend or take new postdoctoral appointments if they are unable to find a faculty job. Most of these appointments offer a nominal salary.

Career Path

A major step in the traditional academic career is attaining tenure. The tenure-track positions are found in four academic ranks: professor, associate professor, assistant professor, and instructor. New tenure-track faculty are usually hired as instructors or assistant professors and must serve a certain period (usually seven years) under term contracts. At the end of the contract period, their record of teaching, research, and overall contribution to the institution is reviewed; tenure is granted if the review is favorable. Those denied tenure are typically asked to leave the college or university.

Tenured professors cannot be fired without just cause and due process. Tenure protects the faculty's academic freedom to teach and conduct research without fear of being fired for advocating unpopular ideas. It also gives both faculty and institutions the stability needed for effective research and teaching and provides financial security for faculty. Some institutions have adopted post-tenure review policies to encourage ongoing evaluation of tenured faculty.

Special Attributes

If you want to be a member of a college's faculty, you should have an inquiring and analytical mind and a strong desire to pursue and disseminate knowledge. You must be able to communicate clearly and logically, both orally and in writing. You should be able to establish rapport with students and, as models for them, be dedicated to the principles of academic integrity and intellectual honesty. Additionally, you must be self-motivated and able to work in an environment where you receive little direct supervision.

Salaries and Fringe Benefits

Earnings vary according to faculty rank and the type of institution, geographic area, and field. By rank, the average salary for professors is more than $65,000; associate professors, $48,000; assistant professors, $40,000; instructors, $30,800; and lecturers, $33,00. Average salaries for faculty in public institutions are lower than those for private independent institutions.

Most faculty members have significant earnings in addition to their base salary. They receive these earnings from consulting, teaching additional courses, research, writing for publication, or other employment, both during the academic year and the summer.

Faculty members enjoy some unique benefits, including access to campus facilities, tuition waivers for dependents, housing and travel allowances, and paid sabbatical leaves. Furthermore, most schools have some funds to support faculty research and development. Part-time faculty have fewer benefits than full-time faculty and usually do not receive health insurance, retirement benefits, or sabbatical leave.

Working as an Assistant Professor

Dr. Angela Keating is a medical doctor and an assistant professor at a major university. Besides handling her own practice with all its responsibilities and chairing a division of a VA hospital, she is responsible for teaching medical students and residents in her office, operating rooms, and in lecture halls. She is also a member of the cabinet for the introduction to clinical medicine course for medical students. Another of her responsibilities is as a member of the medical education review committee responsible for creating goals and objectives to give the faculty more contact with students. The committee makes changes in the curriculum to optimize the education the students receive. A look at the doctor's schedule for one week will let you see how busy she is.

Monday—In the morning, the doctor works as a consultant at a medical center for operative cases. Both a resident and a student typically participate in the surgeries with her. In the afternoon, she has office hours.

Tuesday—The entire day is spent at a VA center in her specialty clinic. While seeing patients, she supervises one first- and one second-year resident and two third-year medical students.

Wednesday—The mornings are set aside for educational conferences for faculty, residents, medical students, and local practitioners. Angela attends these lectures and participates by giving her opinion on various topics from past experience and reviewing studies that have been previously done. Occasionally she will present lectures or mentor the resident who is presenting. Her afternoons are considered her time to do all the odds and ends that weren't done earlier. Angela may meet with various other faculty members regarding research, meet with study patients on clinical research, or work on a proposal for a research protocol. She also uses this day to meet with the two medical students she advises on a rotating eight-week schedule.

Thursday—The entire day is spent in her office seeing patients.

Friday—In the morning, Angela will typically perform surgery at the hospital and go on rounds with her specialty team made up of all levels of residents and medical students. If she is not still in the operating room in the afternoon, she will supervise residents.

Being both a doctor and an assistant professor gives Angela an extremely demanding schedule. Sometimes she may work for two days straight, depending on if she is on call overnight in the hospital. A few times each month, she will be supervising residents and may be up all night and still have to work the next two days.

CAREER PLUSES AND MINUSES

Angela finds it very challenging to find a way to teach while actually caring for patients. She says that one of the things that keeps her going is the challenge of being able to do both well at the same time. She thrives on the fact that she is making a large impact on the quality of life of her patients and on the education experience for her students and residents. The downside of her job is the long hours and having to remain sharp and functional on little or no sleep. Also, she frequently has to correct mistakes that are made by residents or students to safeguard her patients.

Working as a Professor

Dr. James Riley has taught mathematics to more than ten thousand students. His teaching career began as a high school teacher while he was earning his master's in mathematics. When the university suddenly needed a teacher to fill in for an instructor who had gone to Africa to do research, Jim was offered the job because the department head knew him through his studies at the school. Jim admits that this would not happen today. The last time there was an opening in his department, more than one hundred people applied. At first, Jim was not on the university's tenure path as an instructor. After two years, however, he was placed on the tenure track with the understanding that he would get a doctorate. Jim rose through the academic ranks to become an assistant professor, an associate professor, and then a full professor of mathematics.

Each term Jim teaches three classes while most professors teach only two. He teaches three because he enjoys teaching and would feel cheated with fewer classes. The three classes put him in the classroom ten to twelve hours a week. He spends about one hour outside of class in preparation for each hour in class. In addition, he spends about half an hour for each hour in class correcting papers. Other job responsibilities include holding office hours to meet with students, attending departmental and professional meetings, and keeping current with research in mathematics.

Job Opportunities

College and university faculty hold close to nine hundred thousand positions, mainly in public institutions, with about four out of ten working part-time. Some part-timers, known as "adjunct faculty," have primary jobs outside of academia in areas such as government, private industry, or nonprofit research. Others seek full-time faculty jobs but are unable to obtain them due to intense competition for available openings. Some even work part-time in more than one college.

Most faculty members are hired as instructors or assistant professors. Four-year colleges and universities generally only consider doctoral degree holders for full-time, tenure-track positions, but they may hire master's degree holders or doctoral candidates for certain disciplines, such as the arts or for part-time and temporary jobs. However, with increasing competition for available jobs, institutions can be more selective in their hiring practices. Master's degree holders may find it increasingly difficult to obtain employment as they are passed over in favor of candidates holding a Ph.D.

The number of tenure-track positions is expected to decline as institutions rely more heavily on less costly part-time faculty who do not hold tenure-track positions. Consequently, increased reliance on part-time faculty is expected to shrink the total pool of faculty who hold tenure. Some institutions have placed "caps" on the percentage of faculty who can be tenured. Other institutions offer prospective faculty limited term contracts, typically two-, three-, or five-year full-time contracts. They do this in an effort to adapt to changes in their budgets and the size of the student body. These contracts may be terminated or extended at the end of the period. Institutions are not obligated to grant tenure to these contract holders.

More job opportunities will arise through 2006 as a significant number of faculty members retire and enrollment increases. However, in an effort to cut costs, some institutions are expected either to leave these positions vacant or hire part-time, nontenured faculty as replacements. Prospective job applicants have to be prepared to face keen competition for available jobs as growing numbers of Ph.D. graduates, including foreign-born Ph.D.s, vie for fewer full-time openings.

PUBLIC RELATIONS SPECIALISTS

Another area within higher education in which you could obtain employment is public relations. A school's reputation, profitability, and even its continued existence can depend on the degree to which its goals and policies are supported by the public. Specialists in public relations serve as advocates for colleges and universities and other schools and strive to build and maintain positive relationships with the public.

Public relations specialists handle such organizational functions as media, community, consumer, and government relations. Understanding the attitudes and concerns of students, faculty, and groups external to the college is also a vital part of the job. To improve communications, public relations specialists establish and maintain cooperative relationships with representatives of community, consumer, employee, and public interest groups and those in print and broadcast journalism.

These specialists put together information that keeps the students, faculty, and general public aware of the school's policies, activities, and accomplishments. Their work also keeps the administration abreast of public attitudes and concerns of the many groups and organizations with which it must deal.

As a public relations specialist, you would prepare press releases and contact people in the media who might print or broadcast your material. Many radio and television special reports, newspaper stories, and magazine articles about colleges and universities start on the desks of public relations specialists. You would arrange and conduct programs for contact between college representatives and the public. For example, you might set up speaking engagements and prepare the speeches for administrators. As a public relations specialist, you would frequently represent administration at community projects through the use of film, slide, or other visual presentations. In addition, you would write, do research, prepare materials, maintain contacts, and respond to inquiries.

In order to get a public relations job, you will usually need to have a bachelor's degree coupled with public relations experience, usually gained through an internship. You also need creativity, initiative, good judgment, and the ability to express your thoughts clearly. Decision-making, problem-solving, and research skills are also important.

LIBRARIANS

Libraries play an extremely important role in education on college and university campuses as the repository of books, collections, documents, microfilm, microfiche, and other media materials. Both students and their professors rely on their schools' libraries to have the materials essential for research. Some of the world's great libraries are at universities.

Nearly all college libraries contain multiple subdepartments. Some even have several separate libraries. If you were to work in a college library, you could find yourself employed in one of the following sections: circulation, database, acquisitions, collections, cataloging, development, preservation, or systems. Only library clerks and those in activities not directly related to the collection such as development and budget do not have to have degrees in library science. For entry-level librarian positions, you will need to have a master's degree in library science. And in order to get a top administrative job, a Ph.D. in library and information science is advantageous.

CAREER COUNSELORS

Interesting service-related jobs can be found in college and university career centers. These centers will typically employ career and job counselors to help students and alumni develop and fine-tune their job seeking strategies. They help them create resumes and also critique resumes. Some will even set up mock individual and group interviews. These practice interviews enable students to become more comfortable during interviews and teach them what to expect.

When job fairs and company recruiting events come to school campuses, counselors will be at the center of the action. They schedule and place corporate booths, collect the event's registration fees, post maps detailing where each profession will be located, and coordinate the resulting interviews. College career planning and placement counselors may work long and irregular hours during recruiting periods.

FOR MORE INFORMATION

Professional societies generally provide information on academic and nonacademic employment opportunities in their fields. Special publications on higher education like *The Chronicle of*

Higher Education are available in libraries and list specific employment opportunities for faculty.

For information on college student affairs administrators, you should contact:

National Association of Student Personnel Administrators
1875 Connecticut Avenue NW, Suite 418
Washington, DC 20009-5728

For information on collegiate registrars and admissions officers, contact:

American Association of Collegiate Registrars and Admissions Officers
One Dupont Circle NW, Suite 330
Washington, DC 20036-1171

For a list of schools with accredited programs in public relations in their journalism departments, send a stamped, self-addressed envelope to:

Accrediting Council on Education in Journalism and Mass
    Communications
University of Kansas School of Journalism
Stauffer Flint Hall
Lawrence, KS 66045

CHAPTER 7

JOBS AT TRADE SCHOOLS AND COMMUNITY COLLEGES

Some form of formal training after high school has almost become a necessity in order to make a good living. Many high school graduates elect to get this training in trade schools and community colleges rather than in a four-year college program. In the past, trade schools typically offered students training in a career field from welding to baking, while community colleges focused on general education classes leading to a two-year degree and/or entrance into a four-year college program. This is changing as trade schools and community colleges are now moving toward greater similarity in their missions. Trade schools are beginning to offer some general education classes, and community colleges now have strong vocational programs. As the number of students at these schools continues to increase, so will the opportunities for jobs in this area.

TRADE SCHOOLS

Until the start of the nineteenth century, individuals prepared for jobs in industrial and commercial occupations through apprenticeships. That is the way they learned how to shoe horses, repair watches, and lay bricks. As industrialization grew in the nineteenth century, several European countries began offering vocational education in their elementary and secondary schools. In the United States, the federal government began providing aid to public schools to set up trade and industrial courses in 1917. At the same time, private trade schools began to provide training that had been available only through apprenticeships. After World War II, the demand for trained individuals in the new fields of computers, electronics, and medical services plus an accelerated demand for increased training in such areas as welding, car repair, and construction led to the creation of thousands of trade schools from those employing just a few individuals to national chains with thousands of employees. Here is a look at just a few of the trade schools in which you might find employment:

accounting and bookkeeping
acting
acupuncture
advertising
aircraft repair
art
automotive repair
aviation instruction
beauty culture
computers
contractors
cooking
court reporting
data processing
dental assistants
dressmaking
driving instruction
electronics
fashion designing
fashion illustration

film making
financial planning
floral designing and arranging
graphic arts
heavy equipment operation
hotel and motel management
interior decorating
jewelry
medical assistants
merchandising
mortuary science
paralegal
pharmacology
photography
piano tuning and repairing
plumbing
printing
real estate sales
secretarial
security training
tailoring
television and radio broadcasting
travel and tourism
truck driving
veterinary medical assistant
welding
word processing

Job Requirements

If you are interested in teaching at a trade school, you do not have to be a licensed teacher. What you need is expertise in the subject you teach. For example, if you were teaching students who want to receive Microsoft Certified Systems Engineer certification (MCSE), you would need to hold this certification. And if you were teaching courses in welding or baking, you would need to be highly skilled in these areas. In the same way, if you were to work at a nonteaching position such as accounting, marketing, counseling, or administration at a trade school, you would need to have the appropriate education and/or experience for the job.

Job Opportunities

Employers are demanding higher levels of skills for entry-level positions. They are also asking employees to upgrade their skills by keeping abreast of changes in their fields. In addition, businesses are outsourcing training to technical schools. As a result, the number of trade schools is increasing rapidly. Opportunities for jobs are especially good in schools teaching computer technology, automotive mechanics, and medical technology.

Unitek—A Training and Consultant Company

Unitek is located in the heart of Silicon Valley where there is a tremendous demand for qualified computer professionals. This relatively new company, which was established in 1992, provides training in the latest technology to individuals who wish to enter the information technology field as well as to those who wish to upgrade their skills. Each course is designed around real-world problem-solving situations, requiring the latest in top-notch computer networking skills. Most of the courses are taught by experienced Microsoft Certified Trainers, who bring their hands-on work experience to the classroom. Students have the option of taking instructor led, self-study, or web-based training courses. However, using a combination of instructor and home-study is recommended. The courses are offered at two company sites as well as on-site for companies. College credits are offered on the completion of Microsoft technical courses. You can learn more about the large number of courses offered by Unitek by visiting the company web site at www.Unitek.com. The company is a Microsoft Certified Technical Education Center (CTEC) and a Caldera Linux Education Center demonstrating the quality of its instructional program.

Besides being a company that specializes in technical education and certification courses, Unitek offers consulting services. The staff consultants (some are also instructors) provide turnkey solutions for every aspect of information technology design, deployment, and management. The third arm of the company is its information technology contracting services. Unitek provides expert contractors and consultants to solve and support the technical needs of their clients on a short- and long-term basis.

WORKING AS A TRAINING MANAGER

Martin Thisner is the training manager for the Unitek technical education division. In this position, he supervises a staff of salespeople and instructors. His duties include:

- planning and implementing new courses and other training services
- coordinating the efforts of the sales staff who promote Unitek's technical education program to prospective students and corporate clients
- arranging the course schedule, which has different classes each week
- providing instructors for each class
- hiring instructors

Martin entered the job market with a bachelor's degree in economics. His first position was in management consulting, then he entered the human resources department of a large company where he had the opportunity to become involved with training. While working, he earned his M.B.A. in marketing. Martin's strong educational background coupled with his work experiences enabled him to come to Unitek as the marketing director. In this job, he managed the company's advertising, public relations, and market research. As the educational program grew, his job was divided and he became the training manager. A new marketing director was hired to handle those responsibilities.

Martin has always been interested in teaching and initially pursued his M.B.A. with the idea of teaching marketing and business development at night. He feels passionate about education and likes the fact that he is working for a company that is committed to education. Martin describes his work as providing a future to people.

According to Martin, the four skills that you should learn in college are: verbal, written communication, computer, and time management. Then when you enter the workforce, he advises, find a mentor who will serve as your guide in the company where you are working.

Vidal Sassoon

More than fifty years ago, Vidal Sassoon emerged as an industry leader in styling hair. Since then his company has established thirteen schools, academies, and education centers to teach beginners and previously qualified stylists the Sassoon techniques of cutting, styling, and coloring hair. To obtain a license as a hairstylist takes approximately one year of study in the Sassoon education program. However, those stylists who wish to work in one of the twenty-six Sassoon salons located around the world will spend an additional two years as apprentices. Then once they become Sassoon stylists, they will have to learn every new technique, hairstyle, and product developed by the company each year.

WORKING AS A TEACHER

Nicole Tomoda Adams is both a stylist and a teacher in one of Sassoon's three education centers in the United States. The center is located in a salon in a major metropolitan area. Nicole became associated with Sassoon after she had worked in two other salons. At one of the salons, she had been trained to do some teaching. Nicole, however, wanted to become a qualified Sassoon professional, which required a six-month period of retraining. Nicole then became a hairstylist at Sassoon. After six months, she was asked to train as a teacher. At the present time, she works as a stylist four days a week and as an instructor one day a week. Most of her contact with the students is on the floor of the salon, where she supervises their work and makes suggestions. She likes working as an instructor because it gives her a chance to teach the Sassoon techniques to others.

WORKING AS A CREATIVE DIRECTOR

Teachers with outstanding expertise as stylists and educators can become creative directors at Sassoon Education Centers. And this is exactly what Randall Broussard has done. After high school, he trained at the Sassoon academy in Los Angeles following the prescribed path of one year of instruction to get his license and two years of apprenticeship at a Sassoon salon to enhance his skills. After working for several years as a stylist, then as a stylist and teacher, Randall has become the creative director of the salon where Nicole works. In this position, he is in charge of staff development, which involves supervising the education program offered at the salon. Not only does he teach students, he also trains stylists to become teachers. Most of his job is strictly hands-on as he demonstrates techniques and supervises students; however, books and videos are used in the program. As creative director, Randall also is in the charge of image management, which involves checking that all of the staff are meeting the Sassoon standards in their work, dress, and demeanor. In a typical week, he will spend one or two days a week teaching, and the rest of his time is devoted to administrative work and taking care of his clientele.

Hairstylists rarely get to travel. As a creative director, however, Randall has the opportunity to do hair shows throughout the country, to receive additional training in the company's headquarters in London, and to fill in as an instructor in cities across the country.

In any endeavor, you need to have a high level of commitment to succeed in your job, and you must be willing to accept challenges.

COMMUNITY COLLEGES

Community colleges, also called junior colleges, are scarcely one hundred years old; however, they have become so popular that more than 40 percent of all U.S. undergraduates are attending these schools. The enrollment in community colleges exceeds ten million students, and there are now more than one thousand schools. Traditionally, community colleges have provided two years of academic training beyond high school with graduates earning an associate's degree (A.A.). For some students this degree is a final degree; others will complete their education at a four-year college. Besides providing academic training, these colleges also offer training in vocational-technical areas for occupations that do not require a college degree such as welder, dental hygienist, automated systems manager, X-ray technician, auto mechanic, and cosmetologist. In addition, community colleges have adult continuing education classes such as cooking, writing, exercise and physical fitness, photography, and word processing that students take for enjoyment and personal enrichment.

Job Requirements

Training requirements for employment as a teacher at a community college will vary by state, institution, and subject. In general, teachers need work or other experience in their field, and a license or certificate in fields where these are usually required for full professional status. In some cases, a master's or doctoral degree is required to teach nonvocational courses that can be applied toward a four-year degree program. Many vocational teachers do not need to have advanced degrees but draw on their work experience and knowledge. Adult education teachers teaching classes that are taken for interest or enjoyment need only to show a portfolio of work or practical experience in a subject. For example, to secure a job teaching a photography course, an applicant would need to show examples of previous work.

Besides teaching jobs, community colleges will have a similar administrative structure to four-year colleges. This means there will be positions for deans, registrars, admissions officers, department heads, financial aid officers, and their assistants. In addition, community colleges tend to employ counselors to advise their students rather than relying on teachers as four-year colleges do.

Because community colleges accommodate many adults who are working full-time, many jobs, even administrative positions, require working evenings and Saturdays. In addition, a very high percentage of teachers work part-time.

Working Conditions

Because community college teachers and administrators work with mature students, they do not encounter some of the behavioral or social problems found in working with younger students. Teachers, however, have to deal with students at different levels of development who may lack effective study skills and self-confidence and require considerable attention and patience.

Job Opportunities

Rising demand for two-year college programs, vocational training, and adult education courses will spur faster than average employment growth at community colleges. Many of the teachers at these schools work part-time.

Working as a Program Mentor

Community colleges often have interesting positions in innovative areas to meet the special needs of their students. The Program for Adult College Education (PACE) at Diablo Valley College, Pleasant Hill, California, and the Center for Higher Education in San Ramon are community colleges that are designed for working adults and help them complete all required courses in two and a half years by attending class one night a week and on selected weekends. The graduates receive an A.A. degree and then are eligible to transfer as juniors to several local four-year colleges.

One of the individuals helping the students succeed in the PACE program is Ann Uawithya who serves as a mentor. At the same time, she is pursuing her master's degree in business administration. Ann's role is to make sure everyone in the program succeeds by conducting study groups and acting as a liaison between students and instructors. Students in the PACE program are full-time working adults with families who have added another role to their already busy lives. Ann chose to work as a mentor because she wanted to share her education experience and help others travel the path she has traversed successfully as an adult with a family. She knows what it means to juggle studying for a midterm while washing several loads of clothes and preparing dinner. As a mentor, Ann has helped students who have lost their jobs find new ones, arranged car pools, contacted students who were absent, and answered hundreds of questions about college life.

Ann works full-time at the Center for Higher Learning. Besides being a mentor, she also has administrative duties to handle as well as the job postings for the school.

Ann finds it is wonderful to be involved with a group that has grown into an extended family that supports one another. Everyone in the group has inspired her in one way or another. One of the students recently said: "It is both exciting and sad to realize that this will be our last semester together. However, I believe that all of us will keep in touch in the years to come. Thanks to PACE, I can work full-time and get my A.A."

FOR MORE INFORMATION

For positions in trade schools and community colleges, contact these schools directly. For information about adult vocational-technical education teaching positions, contact state departments of vocational-technical education. To learn about adult continuing education teaching positions, contact departments of local government.

CHAPTER 8

JOBS WITH DEPARTMENTS OF EDUCATION AT FEDERAL, STATE, AND COUNTY LEVELS

Since the government is the single largest employer in the United States, there are multiple opportunities for employment at the federal, state, and county levels in departments of education. The variety of jobs is immense. You could find a job at the federal level providing information for a web site, developing objectives for grants, or answering phone questions about financial aid. At the state level, you could be working in the credentials department ensuring that teachers have met licensing requirement or in a school recognition program to identify the best schools. As a county employee, you might be arranging buses for special education students or developing curricular materials for science teachers. For the individual interested in working in education, the greatest variety of jobs lies in the government sector.

UNITED STATES DEPARTMENT OF EDUCATION

Although legislation was passed creating the department of education during the presidency of Andrew Johnson, it was not established as a cabinet-level department until 1980. The department administers and coordinates most federal assistance to education. It also acts as the nation's fact-finding agency, gathering statistics about education and disseminating research findings to educators, policy makers, and the public. The department's programs provide financial assistance to states for such programs as elementary, high school, and college education; vocational and adult education; and the education of the handicapped, gifted, migrants, Native Americans, illiterate, and those whose native language is not English.

The head of the department is the secretary of education, who is supported by deputy undersecretaries for planning, budget, and evaluation; management; and intergovernmental and interagency affairs and a general counsel. Assistant secretaries are in charge of the educational offices for elementary and secondary education, postsecondary education, educational research and improvement, vocational and adult education, legislation, special education, bilingual education, and civil rights.

Finding a Job

The headquarters of the department of education is located in Washington, DC, and has more than three thousand employees. Additionally, there are more than fourteen hundred staff members who work in the department's ten regional offices. If you wish to work in the federal department of education, you should first learn as much as you can about the different agencies. Then by exploring position descriptions within an agency and looking for vacancies, you can find jobs that appeal to you. Much of this research can and should be done on-line.

Applying for a job with the federal government was once a slow, difficult, and confusing process. Applications had to be sent to the Office of Personnel Management (OPM). Today, the process is no longer centralized, and most agencies are doing their own hiring. To get a job can be as simple as finding a vacancy at an agency web site, securing an application on-line, and even filling it out on-line for some positions. Besides finding out about jobs on the Internet, there are hot lines with job information, and job openings are posted in agencies and at federal job information centers. In addition, it often pays to visit an agency and inquire about vacancies or to network with friends employed by the government. Of course, it is essential to complete applications so they showcase your abilities.

Job Opportunities

The focus on improving education has led to new programs and increased job opportunities at the federal level. Within the agencies of the department, there are jobs for every level of worker from those with a high school diploma to those who have doctorates. The department hires statisticians, lawyers, researchers, accountants, administrators, computer experts, writers, educators, legislative assistants, civil rights experts, analysts, budget experts, publication order takers, switchboard operators, public relations and human resources employees, receptionists, administrative assistants, nutritionists, health and safety experts, and many more people with a variety of skills.

Salaries

When you are hired for a position with the federal government, you will probably be placed on the general schedule of federal salary rates by grade and experience. Each year you will undergo a performance evaluation given by your supervisors and will advance based on this evaluation. The general schedule is composed of fifteen grades numbered GS-1 through GS-15. Each grade has a salary range of ten steps that is defined by the level of responsibility, type of work, and the various qualifications required for each position. Employees are typically promoted through steps 1, 2, and 3 at the rate of one step per year. In steps 4, 5, and 6 they move up one step every two years; and in 7, 8, and 9 they move up one step every three years.

Chart of General Schedule Employees and Their Mean Salaries

Grade	# Employees	$ Mean Salary
GS-1	370	13,038
GS-2	2,443	14,880
GS-3	25,764	17,003
GS-4	97,627	19,597
GS-5	166,176	22,133
GS-6	108,556	24,804
GS-7	140,609	27,274
GS-8	41,034	30,892
GS-9	145,110	32,973
GS-10	16,090	37,700
GS-11	210,657	39,925
GS-12	239,332	48,051
GS-13	159,427	58,230
GS-14	85,490	69,539
GS-15	40,325	83,925
Total	1,479,010	Average $39,070

In addition to the general schedule, the federal government has what is called the executive schedule for its senior-level employees working in the executive branch. The executive schedule has a total of five levels. Level I contains all cabinet members. Level II has deputies of major departments and heads of various government agencies. Level III supports nearly all the presidential advisors, chief administrators, and most undersecretaries. Level IV is composed of assistant secretaries, deputy undersecretaries, and general counsels. Level V, the final level, contains deputy assistant secretaries, administrators, and directors of departments such as education.

Chart of the Executive Schedule Employees and Their Salaries

Level	# Employees	$ Mean Salary
I	25	148,400
II	252	133,600
III	84	123,100
IV	32	115,700
V	17	108,200
Total	410	Average $119,561

All federal salaries are reviewed to reflect changes that occur in the consumer price index—a measure of the cost of living. As a federal employee, this review means that your salary will increase at or close to the rate of inflation.

For More Information

The reason people fail to get their dream jobs with the federal government is because they do not understand the hiring process. The following books will make it easier for you to find a job:

Smith, Russ and others. *Federal Applications That Get Results: From SF-171 to Federal-Style Resumes.* Woodbridge, VA: Impact Publications, 1996.

Morgan, Dana and Robert Goldenkoff. *Federal Jobs: The Ultimate Guide.* New York: Macmillan.

Krannich, Ronald L. and Caryl Rae Krannich. *Find a Federal Job Fast!* Woodbridge, VA: Impact Publications, 1995.

On-line, you can discover helpful job information at www.ed.gov/offices/OM/jobhelp.html.

The easiest way to learn more about the department of education is to visit its web site at www.ed.gov.

Information about job vacancies at different education agencies can be found at www.usajobs.opm.gov. Or you can explore a private sector job database such as the Monster Board. The U.S. Department of Education job listings also may be accessed by phone twenty-four hours a day at (202) 401-0559.

STATE BOARDS OF EDUCATION

Within each state there is a board of education that has the authority to make rules, policies, and regulations provided they are in accordance with state and federal laws. The board collaborates with other groups in the development of education programs and is responsible for reviewing rules, contracts, and policy reports prepared by the department of education, the board of regents for the university system, the state board of community colleges, the postsecondary education planning commission, the education practices commission, and many other boards and commissions. In most states, the governor is chairman of the board while the state superintendent or commissioner of education is the secretary and executive officer. There are opportunities to work on the board's staff in support of its activities from legislative initiatives to planning programs.

STATE DEPARTMENTS OF EDUCATION

No two state departments of education are organized in exactly the same way; however, their organizations are quite similar even though some have much larger departments. The departments are in charge of the day-to-day operation of the education system within a state. In doing this, they must follow the laws, regulations, and policies established by the state school boards for all public elementary and secondary schools, community colleges, and four-year colleges and universities. Nearly all state departments of education have two separate offices that set education policy. One office supports elementary, secondary, and special education while the other supports university, college, and community college systems. Private schools also are monitored by the departments of education; however, the rules by which they must abide differ from state to state.

The chief executives in charge of state departments of education typically hold the title of state superintendents of education or commissioners of education. In some states these executives are elected, while in others they are appointed by either the governor or the state board of education. If your goal is to one day have this position, you will need to possess very impressive credentials in the field of education.

Job Opportunities

The size of the school population within a state dictates how large the staff of its department of education will be. Most staffs are currently growing as the state departments have the responsibility of administering many new federal and state programs. Like the federal level, there are job opportunities for individuals with a wide range of skills from administrators to analysts, to architects. You can find out about job openings at state employment offices and listings on the education departments' web sites. Hiring on the state level is generally a very decentralized process, with each department hiring its own personnel. The more you know about the different departments within state departments of education, the easier it will be for you to find the workplace you want. Here is a description of some of the departments found within state departments of education and of some of the jobs in these departments.

The Office of Legislative Affairs

This office is responsible for directing and coordinating all state legislative activities of the department of education. As a staff member, you might take the lead in lobbying the state legislature on behalf of the superintendent and coordinate legislative contacts within the department. Or you might have the responsibility of developing and preparing the superintendent's annual legislative proposals. You could advise and consult with the superintendent and department executives on the progress, status, and requirements of legislative initiatives. Another job possibility is reviewing education programs and proposals to identify areas requiring new or amended legislation.

The Office of Policy Research and Accountability

The state Office of Policy Research and Accountability is responsible for conducting research and data analysis on emerging educational issues. Were you to work in this office, you might assist in providing the superintendent with information necessary for the recommendation of legislation and state board rules that would help to improve the state's education system.

The Office of Communications

The Office of Communications serves as a liaison between the general public and various divisions within the department of education in order to provide assistance in obtaining public information. While working in this office, you might write and distribute press releases and make presentations to various interest groups.

The Office of the General Counsel

If you have an interest in the legal profession, this might be the office for you. The Office of the General Counsel provides legal assistance to the state board of education, superintendent of education, and offices within the department of education. It does this by rendering legal opinions and handling court cases related to educational issues.

The Office of Business and Education Alliances

The Office of Business and Education Alliances is responsible for the coordination and expansion of community involvement in educational programs. Staff in this department focus on effectively using parent and community volunteers, business partnerships, school advisory councils, and family involvement to improve student test scores and graduation rates.

The Office of the Inspector General

The mission of the Office of Inspector General is to assist the state department of education in facilitating its educational needs. Working in this department, you would conduct audits and review existing services. You would investigate and provide assessments of management functions, and you would analyze the efficiency and effectiveness of departmental programs and activities.

The Postsecondary Education Planning Commission

If you were to work on this commission, one of your major responsibilities could be to prepare and update the state's master plan for postsecondary education. You might make recommendations to the state board of education for program contracts with independent institutions. You also could advise the state board on the need for and location of new programs, branch campuses, and centers for public education institutions. You might conduct periodic reviews of the accountability processes and reports of the public and independent postsecondary sectors or review education budget requests for compliance with the state's master plan.

The Office of the Deputy Superintendent

The deputy superintendent or commissioner of education is the direct subordinate to the chief executive of the state department of education. This office is responsible for the overall coordination of planning and all budgetary matters in the department of education. It is comprised of the division of financial services and the division of support services, including the office of student financial assistance. This office is responsible for the development and submission of legislative budgets.

Division of Financial Services—Office of the Comptroller

The Office of the Comptroller provides services in the areas of accounting, financial management information, payroll, grants management, and travel reimbursement to the department's program administrators, employees, and project recipients. Within this office, the strategy and planning unit develops and uses information to prepare both long- and short-range plans and budgets for public schools and related education activities. This is an excellent area for you if you are interested in a job related to financial matters.

The Division of Administration

The division of administration provides administrative support services to the department of education and administers the state's equal educational opportunity program.

The Bureau of General Services

The Bureau of General Services provides assistance to the department of education's staff. If you were working for this bureau, you would help to administer and coordinate emergency management programs and safety programs. You also would oversee procurement, graphics design, records management, property, supply distribution, mail services, and leasing.

Equal Educational Opportunity Program

If you are a strong advocate for human rights, you may want to work for the Equal Educational Opportunity Program. This program seeks to provide an equal opportunity for all students to attain the highest levels of educational achievement. It also seeks to create an environment free of bias, stereotyping, and illegal discrimination. The program's services include consulting and training and technical assistance on a full range of topics dealing with civil rights and equity in education.

Division of Support Services

The Division of Support Services provides leadership, assistance, training, and monitoring services for school districts. The division's major service areas include financial, food and nutrition, and school transportation management.

Division of Human Resource Development

The Division of Human Resource Development provides resources to school districts, universities, and individuals to help ensure that the state's educational workforce is of the highest quality possible. The primary responsibilities of the division include development of standards for the education profession, educator certification and renewal, educator recruitment and awards activities, educator in-service and training, investigation of educator misconduct, and discipline of educators who are found guilty of misconduct.

The Bureau of Teacher Certification

The Bureau of Teacher Certification has responsibility for the certification of instructional staff in the state's public school system. The bureau functions to ensure that the state's educators possess adequate knowledge and relevant subject matter competence and can demonstrate an acceptable level of professional performance.

The Office of Professional Practices Services

The Office of Professional Practices Services is responsible for the review of criminal histories and the investigation of complaints of alleged violations to the state code of ethics.

The Office of Professional Training Services

The Office of Professional Training Services is responsible for providing assistance to school districts, colleges, and universities through the preparation, maintenance, and coordination of a variety of programs and services. These programs are designed to establish a high performing professional education workforce that will directly impact and improve student performance.

Division of Workforce Development

Within the Division of Workforce Development, the Bureau of Program Management and Development offers jobs with a wide variety of responsibilities including administering federal grant programs to school districts, colleges, universities, community-based organizations, correctional institutions, and other eligible agencies. The bureau is also responsible for planning, monitoring, and reporting any improvements that are generated from these funds. In addition, the bureau conducts research to develop innovative state, federal, and private sector grant programs.

Salaries

Most states have established salary scales similar to those of the federal department of education. The same job will not receive the same compensation for equal experience or education in the different states. The salaries can be considerably higher or lower than average salaries for a position depending on the state where you work.

COUNTY DEPARTMENTS OF EDUCATION

Departments of education at the county level are both similar and different to their counterparts on the federal and state levels. First of all, these departments are much closer to the people and schools and are primarily service providers. They also are smaller departments and have fewer responsibilities. The individual departments will typically provide some of the following services as well as many others depending on the size and needs of the student population:

- Business Services: Counties do the payroll and general accounting for school districts as well as budget analysis.
- Alternative Schools: These schools are operated by the county for students who need a special environment in order to receive an education.
- Career Development: Vocational classes in schools are supported by the county through occupational programs.
- Special Education: Counties operate classes and schools for special education and severely handicapped children for school districts that cannot afford or do not have these programs.
- Curriculum and Instruction: All kinds of curriculums are developed for classroom teachers. A resource center has instructional materials for loan.
- Technology Services: Counties help schools set up computer centers and provide support services.
- Transportation Services: Counties provide bus service for special education students.
- School and Community Relations: School-related questions are answered or directed to the appropriate source. Information about schools is provided to the public, and school programs are promoted.

The general hierarchy in county departments of education is similar to that of the federal and state departments of education. An elected or appointed superintendent heads the department of education and has departments handling different administrative responsibilities.

Job Opportunities

The larger the number of students and schools in a county, the greater the number of positions that will be available. Some counties will have just a few positions in a small office, while large urban centers may have departments of education that rival those of some states in size. In the smaller county offices, opportunity for advancement is generally limited, and hiring practices are not standardized. In order to advance professionally, it is usually necessary to move to a larger unit of education government.

CHAPTER 9

EDUCATION RESEARCHERS AND CONSULTANTS

Two careers in education that are not well known are researcher and consultant. Researchers do just as their name suggests, research. They work primarily at education centers associated with universities and also at independent centers where they conduct studies and gather information on a wide variety of topics to improve all aspects of education. Their research is on such projects as multicultural education issues, improving English as a second language instruction, retention, and the impact of homework. Then when a project is completed, results are published as reports, information briefs, and technical assistance documents. Speeches also are given to professional organizations, and journal articles are written. Consultants, on the other hand, are hired to offer specific advice on issues such as where a district should build a new school or the type of computers a school should purchase.

EDUCATION RESEARCHERS

Education researchers look for information about and answers to critical education problems. They hope the data they discover and the proposals they make will create more effective schools in which classroom teaching and learning is strengthened. Researchers work on topics that span the full scope of education. They may study the effects of infant child care, the improvement of first-grade mathematics, or even the uses adults make of their literacy skills. Or they could focus their research on teaching, learning, and assessment as they are applied to mathematics, science, English, the teacher, the learner, the organizational setting, and the curriculum.

Some researchers work on short-term projects to provide information about current education topics and education reform while others do in-depth studies lasting three to five years to provide a more comprehensive picture of a policy, program, or trend. There also are ongoing projects that last for years. For example, researchers investigating the effects of early child care have been studying the same children from infancy, and the children are now in middle school.

In conducting research, the researcher's goal is to discover ways in which improvements in the quality of education will be achieved for everyone. Modern-day researchers attempt to gather and then present their findings in such a way that teaching, learning, curriculum, assessment, and leadership are all affected and united together to ensure effective instruction.

Career Path

Education researchers may work at large public or private centers that are investigating fifty or more projects at a time, smaller centers with fewer projects, or private centers that have a single focus such as researching how students across the country are doing on college admissions tests. The entry-level position for a researcher is project assistant. As an assistant, you would typically work on one project or possibly two collecting and analyzing data. There would be lots of writing in this job. The next step up the career ladder is to project director, running as many as five or six projects. The individual in charge of a center is the director who runs the center with the help of one or more associate directors. Although center and associate directors do research, their primary responsibilities are administrative. Besides directing the activities at centers, center and project directors are often college professors.

Research Methods

Research methods often rely on mathematical models that consist of a set of equations that describe how things happen within an organization. Using models enables researchers to analyze problems and break them into their component parts. They use computers extensively in their work. Many are highly proficient in database collection and management, programming, and the development and use of sophisticated software programs. Many of the models used by researchers are so complicated that only a computer can solve them efficiently.

Regardless of the project, research typically entails a similar set of procedures. Center directors begin the process by outlining the project to a project director, who then formally defines the project and breaks it down into component parts. Project assistants gather information about each of these parts, an action that usually involves consulting a wide variety of sources of information.

With this information in hand, the project assistant is ready to select the most appropriate analytical technique. There may be several techniques that could be used, but virtually all involve the construction of a mathematical model. After building a model, the assistant presents the final work to the project director who coordinates the work of all of the assistants in writing the final report, which is presented to the directors along with recommendations based on the results of the analysis. If a plan of action has been presented, all the researchers may work on its implementation.

Education Requirements

Education researchers come from a wide variety of backgrounds. They may have degrees in sociology, English, law, mathematics, engineering, education, psychology, or social work. As a result, researchers work in an exciting interdisciplinary environment.

You can get a job as a project assistant with a bachelor's degree. However, some assistants have master's degrees or even doctorates. At university research centers, project assistants are often expected to have master's degrees in statistics, education psychology, education measurement, or some related field; possessing course work in mathematics is also beneficial. Plus, it is very helpful to have prior work experience in analyzing data and using statistical models and large databases. Both project directors and center directors will have doctorates.

Special Attributes

Researchers must be able to think logically and work well with people. Since so much writing is involved in the preparation of reports, they need to have excellent writing skills. Verbal skills also are quite important in communicating with each other on the progress of a project. In addition, it is important to be able to work with others as many projects require team efforts. Beginning researchers usually do routine work under the supervision of those who are more experienced. As they gain knowledge and experience, they are assigned more complex tasks, with greater autonomy to design models and solve problems. Therefore, it is necessary to be able to work independently.

Working as a Project Assistant

Stephanie Cawthom works part-time as a project assistant at a research center located on the campus of a major university. The center, however, is not part of the university even though the directors are university professors. Like many of the other project assistants, Stephanie is studying for her doctorate and also working as a teaching assistant. Her background is ideal for this job as she holds bachelor's and master's degrees in psychology, which require a thorough knowledge of statistical analysis. In addition, she worked for three years as a consultant at a small education consulting firm.

Stephanie is currently working on two research projects at the center. One project involves investigating the effects a new program will have on improving student achievement in a very large urban school district. Six principal investigators are directing this project, and fourteen project assistants are working on subcomponents of the project. Stephanie's component is special education, and she is looking at the effect the program will have on all children with disabilities. In order to do this research job she is interviewing teachers and parents, observing classrooms, looking at test accommodations for special education students, working with district guidelines, studying student scores, and gathering regular classroom teachers' opinions on having special education students in their classrooms. Her inquiry is based upon research methods of the field, and she is guided by the literature on the topic. Stephanie's second project involves doing statistical analysis of research done on the effects of Down's syndrome on families. She is the database manager for this project.

Job Opportunities

Employment opportunities for education researchers will grow at a rate above average through 2006 because demand for the information they provide is increasing. As primary and secondary school districts reorganize and reevaluate their current level of success, researchers will be called upon to analyze and help create more effective learning centers. Many of the job opportunities will be in the rapidly growing number of small firms that provide this service.

CONSULTANTS

An education consultant's job is to analyze and suggest solutions to questions and problems posed by clients. For example, a school district may need help in projecting the costs of reducing class size. Or in another case, a school may question the effectiveness of a bilingual education program. The work of consultants varies with each client and from project to project. Some projects require a team of consultants, each specializing in one area while others require consultants to work independently. In general, education consultants first collect, review, and analyze information. They then make recommendations to clients and may assist in the implementation of their proposals.

Both public and private educational organizations, especially school districts, use consultants for a variety of reasons. Some don't have the internal resources needed to handle a project; others need a consultant's expertise to determine what resources will be required and what problems may be encountered if they pursue a particular path such as changing a high school to a block scheduling plan.

Firms providing consulting services range in size from a single practitioner to large organizations employing many consultants. Consulting services often are provided on a contract basis. The consultant is hired to develop solutions to a problem. Once they have decided on a course of action, consultants report their findings and recommendations to the client in writing and frequently through oral presentations. For some projects, this is all that is required. For others, consultants assist in the implementation of their suggestions.

Job Requirements

Entry-level applicants at consulting firms are expected to have bachelor's degrees; however, master's degrees are preferred. The area of concentration is not important; liberal arts majors can find jobs as consultants. Entry-level consultants, called analysts, learn their work on the job, working at first with middle-level managers in large firms and owners at small firms.

Career Path

As analysts gain experience, they often become solely responsible for one specific project. In large consulting firms, analysts can advance to positions as middle-level managers and then senior managers. At the senior level, consultants may supervise lower-level workers and become increasingly involved in seeking out new business. Others with entrepreneurial ambitions may open their own firms.

Special Attributes

Consultants often work with little or no supervision, so they should be self-motivated and disciplined. Analytical skills, the ability to get along with a wide range of people, and strong oral and written communication skills are essential to being successful consultants. They also should possess good judgment, know how to manage time well, and have creativity in developing solutions to problems.

Salaries and Fringe Benefits

Salaries for consultants vary widely by experience, education, and employer. The average salary for full-time workers is approximately $39,500 per year. The middle 50 percent earn between $30,000 and $60,000, and the top 10 percent will earn more than $80,000. Earnings—including bonuses and/or profit sharing—in member firms average about $35,000 for entry-level consultants, $50,000 for management consultants, $74,000 for senior consultants, $91,000 for junior partners, and $167,000 for senior partners. The average annual salary for management analysts in the federal government in nonsupervisory, supervisory, and managerial positions is approximately $55,000.

Typical benefits for salaried analysts and consultants include health and life insurance, a retirement plan, vacation and sick leave, profit sharing, and bonuses for outstanding work. In addition, all travel expenses are usually reimbursed by the employer. Self-employed consultants have to maintain their own office and provide their own benefits.

Typically, analysts and consultants work at least forty hours a week. Uncompensated overtime is common, especially when project deadlines are near. Since they must spend a significant portion of their time with clients, they travel frequently. Self-employed consultants can define their own hours and work at home. On the other hand, their livelihood depends on their ability to maintain and expand their client base.

Working as a Consultant in Private Practice

Glenis Benson is an educational psychologist who runs her own private consultation business for individuals with Autism Spectrum Disorders (ASD). In order to bring in business, Glenis advertises through the Autism Society via their newsletter and their web site. Her advertisements let potential clients know that she is available for consultation for persons with this disorder.

Glenis has a rather atypical method for consulting with the parents, teachers, administrators, and universities who are her clients. The novelty of her consultation is that *she goes to the client.* Most professionals will see the child with ASD in their offices, an action that Glenis believes totally ignores the individual in the context in which he or she spends the majority of time. By taking her consultation on the road, she is able to meet with more people and see a child where he or she needs to be seen. Glenis also chats with parents and teachers via the Internet and reviews videotapes of children that parents send her.

In order to provide state-of-the art consultation, Glenis must remain current with the latest research and information in her field. She reads journals, keeps abreast of conference topics, and buys tapes of the conference sessions she thinks will be most useful. Glenis also has memberships in the Autism Society of America and the American Speech and Hearing Association.

CAREER PATH

After obtaining her undergraduate degree in psychology, Glenis worked in a private school for children with autism for three years. Next, she went to work for the provincial government (Canada) consulting for children with autism in their homes and schools. Upon earning her master's degree, in which she conducted research on individuals with high-functioning autism, she consulted for a large city school district in western Canada. Her team was responsible for consultation for half of the province, an area equivalent to the size of six to eight states. Glenis became the director of the autism program after receiving her doctorate. Next, she became an adjunct member of the faculty at the University of Louisville, where she taught a distance education course on autism. She is now a private consultant.

Glenis loves her job and the wonderful people with whom she works. She has no pressure and no bosses and is able to do what she wants and accept or pass on consulting jobs. For her, one of the best parts of this job is being able to spend time with her family. In the future, Glenis would consider doing research in a "fellow appointment" at a nearby research facility. Never again will she seek another tenure-track faculty position, as she believes there is too much pressure for far too little remuneration. In the future, she would like to add larger clients including the state and school districts to her practice.

Glenis believes that it is very important to love your work and adds that people who become consultants do so because they feel so passionate about it. She also says that the more education you have, the more autonomy and respect you will be afforded. Glenis adds that in order to be successful you must have analyzed your clients and discerned what it is that they want from you.

Working as a Consultant for a Small Firm

Before becoming an education researcher, Stephanie Cawthon, whose career was described earlier in the chapter, was an education consultant. The small private firm where she worked immediately after graduating from college with her master's degree, specialized in school facility planning. The three owners were real hands-on people who clearly spelled out what Stephanie's role would be on every project. Typically, she would gather information and then write reports. She would usually be working on three or more projects at a time. The only other employees at the firm were another consultant and a secretary.

Much of Stephanie's work centered around helping school districts project future enrollment and make plans to accommodate the students. This would involve such things as analyzing how many students a district would have in fifteen years, determining how many schools were needed and how they should be configured, redrawing school boundaries, and working with parents to establish bus routes. As in all consultant jobs, considerable computer expertise was required. Stephanie helped write a software program to assist schools in projecting enrollment. She wrote the user manuals and also taught school personnel how to use the program.

Stephanie learned how to be an education consultant on the job. She believes that this entry-level job in consulting gave her excellent training for any work she may do in the future. She advises future consultants to hone their writing skills while in college because being an effective writer is essential in this career.

Job Opportunities

A high percentage of education consultants are self-employed, partly because business start-up costs are low. Self-employed consultants also can share office space, administrative help, and other resources with other self-employed consultants or small consulting firms, thus reducing overhead costs. Employment of consultants is expected to grow faster than average for all occupations through the year 2006 as more and more school districts increasingly rely on outside expertise to improve the performance of their schools. Growth is expected not only in very large consulting firms, but also in smaller niche consulting firms whose consultants specialize in specific areas of expertise.

In spite of projected rapid employment growth, competition for jobs as analysts and consultants is expected to be keen. Consultants can come from such diverse educational backgrounds that the pool of applicants from which employers can hire is quite large.

Additionally, the independent and challenging nature of the work, combined with high earnings potential, make this occupation attractive to many. Job opportunities are expected to be best for those with a graduate degree.

For More Career Information

For information about career opportunities in consulting contact:

Association of Management Consulting Firms
521 Fifth Avenue, 35th Floor
New York, NY 10175-3598

For information about a career as a county or state government consultant, contact your county or state employment service.

CHAPTER 10

LEARNING AND TEST PREPARATION CENTERS AND TUTORING

With crowded classrooms and tight school budgets, more and more children are falling behind in school and are unable to get the help they need. Other children need help in catching up to their classmates because public schools have started to set higher standards for promotion from one grade to the next and for graduation. Also, parents are seeking help for their gifted children who are not being challenged in the regular classroom setting. And because the college experience has become a requirement for so many careers, high school students are looking for ways to receive good scores on college admissions tests. The increasing number of children who need help to get the best possible education has created a burgeoning demand for learning and test preparation centers and private tutors. Here is an opportunity to be involved in education in a field that is growing rapidly.

THE BUSINESS OF LEARNING CENTERS

Open the Yellow Pages, look under "tutoring," and you will find many learning centers. Most of these centers are located in suburban areas; however, some are now running programs in public schools. There are large chains such as Sylvan Learning Centers,

Huntington Learning Centers, Kumon Math & Reading Centers, and SCORE! Educational Centers. All of these chains are expanding rapidly. While most of the chains franchise the local centers, some companies own local centers and all SCORE! centers are corporate-owned. At the same time, there are many independent and nonprofit groups running one or more centers.

Sylvan Learning Centers

Sylvan Learning Centers is the largest of the educational chains with more than seven hundred centers. Although the cornerstone of the company is the learning centers, the company is involved in other education-related enterprises. It has partnerships with both public and private school districts to provide basic skills instruction and specialized services to economically disadvantaged students. The Sylvan Prometric division delivers computer-based testing for professional certification, academic admissions, and information technology programs. Sylvan subsidiaries provide corporate consulting, training, and professional development services. Overall, this huge provider of educational services to families, schools, and industries has more than five thousand educational and testing centers around the globe offering a variety of jobs to people who want careers in the education arena.

Sylvan Learning Centers offer supplemental education to provide enrichment and remediation in:

beginning reading
accelerated reading
academic reading
Sylvan CLEAR writing
basic mathematics
algebra
geometry
study skills

advanced reading skills
academic enrichment
SAT/ACT college
Advanced Youth Scholars Program (with the Johns Hopkins University)
certified high school courses for credit in geometry, algebra 1–2, trigonometry, precalculus, and English, 9, 10, 11.

At the core of every Sylvan program is the "mastery learning" approach. It begins with a diagnostic assessment to determine a student's current capabilities. Then comes a tailored instruction program that moves the student through a hierarchy of progressively difficult tasks to reach a new level of learning, with rewards for effort and accomplishment at each stage. After every twelve hours of instruction, there is a parent conference to discuss the child's progress.

JOBS AT SYLVAN LEARNING CENTERS

The typical jobs at Sylvan Learning Centers are: teacher, director of education, and center director. At some centers, there is administrative staff who assist in the running of the center.

Teachers are part-time employees who work after school and on Saturdays during the school year and throughout the day in the summer. They must be certified teachers. Sylvan teachers are guaranteed a small student/teacher ratio (usually 3:1) and follow a tailored instruction program for each student.

Directors of Education must hold teacher certification, and previous teaching experience is preferred. They are responsible for hiring teachers, creating weekly testing schedules, and ensuring the educational quality of each student's curriculum. A center, especially larger ones, may have more than one director of education for this full-time position.

Center Directors are expected to have experience in the education field. They are responsible for handling the day-to-day management of center staff, increasing student enrollment, marketing the center, and fostering relationships with parents and school. This is a full-time position.

WORKING AS A TEACHER AND DIRECTOR OF EDUCATION

Melinda Adam had just graduated from college with a degree in education when she started working at a Sylvan Learning Center as a teacher. Before she began to work with the students, she was trained on-site in the Sylvan "mastery learning" program. Once she began to tutor, she helped students with math, reading, algebra, writing, and study skills. Typically, she would work fifteen hours a week. Although Melinda would usually have three students at her table, she worked with each one individually while the others handled assignments that she had given them. For each student she had a binder that detailed exactly how she would help that student. It was easy to get the students started on the day's lessons as they usually didn't arrive simultaneously. At the end of each group session, she would put notes on each student's work in his or her binder.

Melinda really liked doing small group instruction. She was able to get a sense of where each student needed help, which is not easy to do in a class with thirty or more students. Also, she liked not having to take work home as teachers in traditional classrooms must do.

After working at the learning center for two months, Melinda climbed the career ladder to become the director of education. In this job, she will occasionally substitute for absent teachers; however, her major responsibilities in this full-time job include: managing the students' programs (giving diagnostic tests and setting up individual learning programs); scheduling teachers; training teachers; doing parent conferences; and staying on top of supplies.

As part of her job, Melinda also attends ongoing training sessions to enhance her skills as a director of education. She is very enthusiastic about her job because she believes she is truly helping children. Melinda also enjoys having both administrative and teaching tasks.

Huntington Learning Centers

Huntington Learning Centers is another very large chain with hundreds of centers. It is the oldest in the United States offering supplemental education. Huntington features a diagnostic prescriptive approach that begins with a series of diagnostic tests to demonstrate a student's abilities and identify problem areas. Then a comprehensive program of instruction is set up for each student. Unlike other programs, which focus on helping a student in a particular subject, Huntington works on helping children improve in all areas. For example, in a typical one-and-a-half-hour session, a student has both reading and math instruction. Besides remedial programs, Huntington offers preparation for college admissions tests.

WORKING AS A HUNTINGTON CENTER DIRECTOR/OWNER

Penny Haeberlin is the director of a Huntington Learning Center in the suburbs of a very large metropolitan area. As director, she oversees the operation of the center, which includes directing the staff, meeting with parents, promoting the center, and dealing with all the financial aspects of operating a center. To handle all the administrative duties for this center, which typically works with more than two hundred students in a year who stay an average of eight to ten months, she has an assistant director of administration. Penny's director of education, a credentialed teacher and full-time employee, handles the educational program, which includes testing students, developing an individualized program for each student, holding conferences with parents, training teachers, and supervising the teaching floor. The educational director is assisted by a full-time assistant director of education. The teaching staff at this center includes approximately fifteen part-time, credentialed teachers.

Besides serving as the center's director, Penny is also the owner. Her background was in business when she decided to purchase a franchise to operate a Huntington Learning Center. She went to company headquarters for training in operating a center. Since her initial training, she participates at least once a year in a regional training session to ensure that her center keeps to the high standards of the chain. Penny has found owning a center to be a very rewarding career. Parents are constantly thanking her for giving their children a second chance to succeed in school. Plus, she finds it gratifying to make a difference in a child's life.

Kumon Math & Reading Centers

The Kumon program was started in Japan more than forty years ago. It is not a tutoring program like those in most learning centers. Instead, it focuses on independent learning. After diagnostic tests are given to pinpoint their level of ability in basic skills, students are given worksheets that they will find easy to complete. Students practice and rework incorrect answers until they achieve 100 percent before going onto the next level. Most students visit Kumon Math & Reading Centers twice a week. They hand in completed homework assignments and then do timed worksheets under the supervision of the Kumon instructor. Their work is graded by the instructor, and they don't leave the center until all mistakes are corrected. All students are given homework assignments to be done each day until the next class session.

JOB OPPORTUNITIES AT KUMON

All Kumon centers are owned by franchisees who purchase the franchise for a small, very affordable cost and then pay the company a royalty per student per month. Many of the franchisees also serve as the directors of their centers and as Kumon instructors. Besides employing instructors, some centers also hire assistants to answer the phone. Because Kumon instructors work with so many students, there are fewer jobs than at other learning centers. It is not necessary to be a credentialed teacher to be a Kumon instructor.

SCORE! Educational Centers

SCORE! Educational Centers have a sports theme, and a great effort is put into making the time spent at SCORE! a fun activity. For example, when students do well on a lesson, they take shots at a basketball hoop, and the individuals guiding the students through the computerized language arts and math curriculum are referred to as coaches. SCORE! is designed for students who need help at school as well as straight-A students between the ages of four and fourteen. Before students begin a computerized program, their skills are evaluated so they will be working at an appropriate level of difficulty.

JOB OPPORTUNITIES AT SCORE! CENTERS

The corporate offices of SCORE! hire the full-time center employees. Part-time employees are hired by center directors.

Assistant Coaches are part-time employees, often high school students. They work with from ten to twenty students who are on computers answering questions and helping the students shoot baskets.

Coaches are full-time employees who serve as center directors. Depending on the size of the center, there may be three to five coaches. They do not need to be certified teachers but must be college graduates. Coaches diagnose the capabilities of the students and monitor their progress, help students build critical skills, talk with parents, market the center, and manage the business and financial performance of a center.

Senior Directors are in charge of several centers. Typically, they have advanced to this position from being a coach at a center.

More Career Opportunities

Job opportunities at learning centers are definitely not limited to working at a center associated with a chain—there are thousands of independent learning centers. While some may have only a few employees, many employ a substantial number of people. When investigating a career with learning centers, you need to look beyond the local center to the regional and national offices of the chains. Because the operation and franchising of hundreds of learning centers is a large business, they offer jobs in management, sales, marketing, accounting, training, and administration. What's more, because this field is rapidly expanding, future opportunities for employment and climbing the career ladder are excellent in this relatively new business.

TEST PREPARATION CENTERS

One of the hurdles that high school students have to pass to be admitted to most colleges is getting a good score on college admissions tests. Again, when they seek admission to graduate school, they need high scores on such tests as the LSAT, MCAT,

GMAT, and GRE. And finally, it is necessary to pass standardized tests to enter many professions. Because all of these tests play a very important role in students' lives, a great number take courses to prepare for them. Many learning centers, test preparation companies, and even individuals provide courses to prepare for the PSAT, SAT, and ACT. However, the two major companies with hundreds of locations across the country and abroad offering test preparation courses for college, graduate school, and professions are Kaplan and The Princeton Review.

Kaplan Educational Centers

Kaplan has helped more than three million students in its test preparation courses over the past sixty years. Today, live courses are given at twelve hundred locations throughout the world. It is not easy to be a Kaplan teacher—usually a part-time position. Applicants have to demonstrate top standardized test scores and audition for the position by giving a brief presentation. Then successful applicants are coached until they are prepared to enter the classroom. Opportunities at Kaplan go far beyond being a teacher. There are jobs for area directors, center managers, assistant center managers, directors of academic development, professional development curriculum managers, associate center managers, marketing coordinators, telesales representatives, academic managers, academic coordinators, marketing assistants, general managers, and many other positions. Most of these jobs require a bachelor's degree.

The Princeton Review

The Princeton Review began in 1981 with only fifteen students. Today, the company helps more than seventy-five thousand students each year excel on standardized tests at the high school, college, and professional levels. Like Kaplan, teachers at The Princeton Review must have scored very high in the standardized test they might be teaching. Also, they have to demonstrate their aptitude for teaching at an audition. Besides teachers who are typically part-timers, The Princeton Review employs hundreds of full-time employees to run the company. They have jobs for accountants, computer experts, salespeople, artists, and managers.

TUTORING

The idea of working one-on-one with a student is definitely not a new one. Alexander the Great, who conquered much of the known world more than twenty-five hundred years ago, was tutored by Aristotle. Today, more than 42 percent of Americans believe there is a "great need" for children to receive private tutoring outside school, according to a *Newsweek* poll. Although it isn't essential to have an education degree or to have been a teacher for this profession, most tutors have been teachers. Some high school tutors, however, only have expertise in a particular subject such as languages or mathematics.

Some tutors give tests to diagnose the difficulties of the students they tutor while others receive diagnoses from teachers, psychologists, and consultants. Elementary school tutors usually concentrate on helping children acquire basic skills in reading, writing, and mathematics and also spend considerable time teaching study skills. Middle school and high school tutors will typically work with a student on a single subject such as English or algebra.

Some tutors work in learning centers; however, most tutors either set up businesses in their own homes or go to the homes of individual students. Tutors running their own businesses usually need to invest in a wide range of curriculum materials in order to help their individual clients. If you decide on a career as a tutor, you should expect to work afternoons, evenings, and weekends when children are not in school. Most tutors work part-time, although it is possible to have a full-time career as a tutor. What you earn as a tutor depends on the number of clients you have, your expertise, and the area where you live. Tutors can expect to earn between $15 to $50 an hour. A tutor with unusual expertise might command as much as $70 an hour.

Working as a Tutor

Pennie Needham brings exceptional qualifications to her job as a tutor. Not only has she taught in classrooms from elementary school through college, she also has special education credentials that attest to her skills in diagnosing the educational problems of her clients. When clients are referred to her, Pennie begins by giving diagnostic tests to pinpoint exactly what the child's weaknesses and strengths are. Then she holds a conference with the parents to set up a plan to help the child. She works with each client for only one hour a week; however, it is really more than an hour because she has to prepare work for each session as well as communicate with parents and teachers about how the child is progressing. Pennie schedules her clients after school during the week. In the summer, they can visit earlier in the day. She finds being a tutor a very satisfying career because she is really helping children.

Pennie advises prospective tutors to investigate this career while still in school by serving as a peer tutor to classmates.

FOR MORE INFORMATION

To find out about opportunities to work in large national learning centers, contact:

Sylvan Learning Centers
   Phone: 1-877-29-TEACH
   Web site: www.educate.com

Huntington Learning Centers
   Phone: 1-800-226-5327
   Web site: www.huntingtonlearning.com

Kumon Math & Reading Centers
   Phone: 1-800-222-6284
   Web site: www.kumon.com

SCORE! Educational Centers
   Phone: 1-800-497-2673
   Web site: www.kaplan.com

For more information about working at a test preparation center, contact:

Kaplan Educational Centers
   Phone: 1-800-527-8378
   Web site: www.kaplan.com

The Princeton Review
   Phone: 1-800-273-8439
   Web site: www.review.com

CHAPTER 11

MORE GREAT JOBS IN EDUCATION

More job opportunities exist in activities that support education. Classroom teachers at all levels rely on textbooks and multimedia materials in educating their students. Teachers and administrators need standardized tests to measure students' progress. Professional organizations offer valuable services to teachers and administrators. Unions negotiate teacher contracts with school boards. All of these activities and many others provide additional job opportunities for those who want to be associated with education. In addition, more jobs exist in giving formal instruction in skills such as dancing, acting, playing tennis, and flower arranging. Many people have started schools to teach these skills. This chapter presents a few more job opportunities in the field of education.

TEXTBOOK WRITERS

Writing textbooks is usually a part-time job for college professors and teachers. Many college professors actually write the textbooks used in their classes, while textbooks used in elementary, middle, and high school classes are often written by a team of writers. No matter who writes a textbook, he or she will be an expert in that subject. Once a textbook is written, the authors will typically be asked to revise it when the textbook needs to be updated.

Textbook authors do not receive salaries; instead they get royalties on the sales of their books. Occasionally, for small projects, they will receive a lump-sum payment for a work.

SUPPLEMENTARY MATERIALS WRITERS

Students do not just use textbooks. At some schools, they may complete as many as one thousand worksheets in a year. In addition, most students use workbooks and an ever-changing variety of supplementary materials. These materials are produced by both large and small educational publishing houses. Many teachers supplement their salaries by writing this material; however, there are some writers who work full-time in this area. They will usually create materials for several publishers.

NEWSPAPER, MAGAZINE, AND JOURNAL WRITERS

Education is a very hot topic today in both newspapers and magazines. While magazines usually use freelance authors to produce education stories, larger newspapers have full-time education reporters to write stories about local, state, and national issues and events. For these jobs, journalistic skill is more important than having a background in education. Education jobs at newspapers are not limited to reporting jobs. Many newspapers have one or more individuals working full-time in their Newspaper in Education programs, which are designed to promote students' interest in reading the newspaper. These people design materials that are sent out to schools, make sure schools get newspapers, and coordinate the activities for the nationwide Newspaper in Education week every March.

Within the field of education, there are a great number of professional associations such as the National Council of Teachers of Mathematics, the International Reading Association, and the Association of Elementary School Principals. Many of these associations publish journals with articles usually written by educators.

EDITORS

Editors who work at publishing houses, magazines, and journals that publish educational materials plan the contents of the materials and supervise their preparation. They decide what will appeal to readers, assign topics to writers, and oversee the production of publications. They almost always review, rewrite, and edit the work of writers. Editors also hire writers, plan budgets, and negotiate contracts with freelance writers. In small organizations, a single editor may do everything. In larger ones, there are far more job opportunities as they have executive editors, assistant editors, editorial assistants, copy editors, and production assistants. Jobs as assistants are entry-level jobs. For all of these jobs, a bachelor's degree in English or journalism is the most common prerequisite.

Entry-level salaries for editorial assistants are slightly more than $21,000 per year. After five years, they can expect to be earning more than $30,000 a year.

MORE JOBS AT EDUCATION PUBLISHING HOUSES

While some publishers of educational materials have just a few employees, many employ hundreds of people. Within the larger organizations there are the same types of jobs as in companies not focused on selling education products: management, public relations, legal, accounting, marketing, information systems, and product development. There is also frequently a large sales force.

Sales representatives try to sell books, workbooks, videos, games, and other educational materials to schools. In order to do this, they must be able to explain the educational benefits of their products to teachers, department chairpersons, principals, curriculum directors, and school boards. For this reason, many sales representatives are former teachers. They spend most of their workdays visiting schools and working in booths at conventions. Their territories may be a large metropolitan area, part of a state, an entire state, or several states. Although most sales representatives work for a company and sell only its products, some work independently and sell the products of several companies.

Most sales representatives earn a combination of salary and commission or salary plus bonus and are usually reimbursed for expenses such as transportation costs, meals, hotels, and entertaining clients. The average annual income of sales representatives is more than $36,000 a year.

TEST COMPANIES

Most school districts give their students standardized tests at least once a year to see how their achievement matches up to that of other students across the country. These tests are created by testing companies and the testing departments of major book publishers. The test organizations also score the tests and develop national norms so student achievement can be compared. Individuals who have jobs directly involved with the creation of standardized tests have to be experts in tests and measurements as well as the subject matter being tested.

Standardized achievement tests are definitely not the only tests developed by testing companies. Testing is a big business with job opportunities for those who can create, score, administer, norm, and even sell tests. There are diagnostic tests to determine the areas in mathematics and reading that are causing students or even adults difficulty. IQ tests measure an individual's innate capabilities while aptitude tests reflect their interests, especially career interests. In addition, psychological tests or inventories describe people's mental states. And there are tests to certify professional competence in many fields from law, medicine, and teaching to welding and computer skills.

Two of the largest testing companies are involved with college admission testing programs. The College Board is the creator of the PSAT, SAT I, SAT II: Subject Tests, as well as AP examinations. ACT, Inc. produces PLAN and the ACT.

PROFESSIONAL ORGANIZATIONS AND UNIONS

Many teachers belong to professional organizations associated with the subjects they teach such as the International Reading Association and the National Council of Teachers of Mathematics, while others belong to associations related to their jobs like the National Association of Secondary School Principals. These associations produce books, journals, and newsletters and have local, regional, and national conventions to keep their members up to date on what is happening in education. Many of these organizations also offer membership services from job information to workshops. All offer a variety of jobs associated in some way with education.

More than half of all teachers belong to unions—mainly the American Federation of Teachers and the National Education Association. These unions bargain with school systems over wages, hours, and the terms and conditions of employment and engage in lobbying activities. They are large organizations with local, state, and national offices offering many job opportunities.

INTERNET COMPANIES

The newest jobs in education are with web-based companies that are designed specifically for students, parents, and teachers. They offer advice and information for parents, homework and research help for students, and curriculum suggestions for teachers on the Internet. These cyber companies have jobs for web site creators as well as for editors and other education experts. Visit www.familyeducation.com to see all the services one of these companies offers as well as to explore job possibilities.

SPEAKERS

Schools often want to bring in speakers to talk to students at assemblies and to teachers at professional meetings. One speaker might travel across the country showing children how to enjoy poetry and teaching them to write poems. Another might speak to teachers about new classroom management techniques. They also will speak on education topics at conventions and other professional meetings. These speakers usually find their jobs through speakers' bureaus.

SCHOOL SECRETARIES

School secretaries hold extremely important jobs. They often are the first contact people have with a school as they greet visitors and answer phone calls. Their job duties may include: keeping records, filing reports, finding substitute teachers, duplicating materials, writing letters, helping sick children, keeping track of funds, scheduling conferences, preparing newsletters and programs, scheduling events in meeting rooms and on athletic fields, coordinating volunteer activities, and serving as an unofficial guidance counselor. To handle this job, it is essential to have solid organizational and management skills, an ability to work well with others, and strong computer skills. The larger a school is, the greater the number of secretaries and the more specialized their duties become.

The salaries of school secretaries vary a great deal depending on the area of the country and level of responsibility. Beginning secretaries with limited experience will start at about $20,000 a year.

MEDIA SPECIALISTS

Almost every school has a librarian, often called a media specialist. This is a most appropriate title as today's librarians handle far more than the traditional library books, newspapers, and periodicals. School librarians now have to deal with videos, tapes, CD-ROMs, computers, and the Internet. Their duties include helping students and teachers find the information they need, teaching students how to use the library, acquiring and cataloging new materials, and overseeing the management of the library, which may include both paid and volunteer assistants.

Job requirements vary widely depending on where a school librarian is employed. Most states require librarians to be certified as teachers and have courses in library science. In some states, a master's degree in library science with a library media specialization or a master's in education with a specialty in school library media or education media is needed.

SCHOOLS THAT TEACH SKILLS

Besides formal academic schools, every community has schools that teach both children and adults skills for their personal enjoyment and interests. There are schools for teaching bridge, dancing, all types of sports, cooking, flower arranging, painting, piano and violin, and much more. In some of these schools, the owner is the teacher and does all of the other tasks associated with running a business; others have several employees who are mostly teachers working part-time. There are a few national chains in this area, providing instruction in such skills as dancing and sports.

EDUCATION SUPPLY AND LEARNING STORES

Education supply stores provide teachers and schools with paper, chalk, pencils and pens, magnetic letters, poster boards, grading and lesson plan books, and all the other materials used in classrooms. In recent years, learning stores have opened that sell materials such as books, toys, games, and computer software that children can use for fun and to improve their educational skills. Both supply and learning stores need salespeople and management staff who are acquainted with the educational needs of their customers.

A SOLID CAREER CHOICE

To function well in today's complex world, everyone needs to know a great deal. Furthermore, the key to continual progress toward an even better world lies in education. When you choose a career in education, you not only benefit individuals but also society. What is so exciting about the field of education is the vast number of job opportunities that let you contribute to helping people get more out of life.